ID0982832

The Man in The Ditch

A Redemption Story for Today

Mike H. Bassett

The Man in The Ditch, LLC

Published by The Man in The Ditch, LLC
Dallas, Texas
www.themanintheditch.com

Cover art by Dust Devil Press, LLC

ISBN: 978-1-7372351-0-1

To Liz, C.J., and Kyle. My people. Back to back. To Hell and back.

Everything can be taken from a man but one thing: the last of the human freedoms—to choose one's attitude in any given set of circumstances, to choose one's own way.

~ Viktor Frankl, Man's Search for Meaning

Lloyd Christmas: What are the chances of a guy like you and a girl like me...ending up together?

Mary Swanson: Not good.

Lloyd: Not good like one in a hundred?

Mary: I'd say more like one in a million.

Lloyd: So you're telling me there's a chance?

~ *Jim Carey and Lauren Holly* in Dumb and Dumber

Contents

Introduction

It is not the critic who counts; not the man who points out how the strong man stumbles, or where the doer of deeds could have done them better. The credit belongs to the man who is actually in the arena, whose face is marred by dust and sweat and blood; who strives valiantly; who errs, who comes up short again and again, because there is no effort without error and shortcoming[.]

~ **Theodore Roosevelt**

Monday, February 4, 2002, was a watershed moment: The Bassett Firm opened its doors and I found myself at the helm of my very own law practice. This was a dream I'd first conceived as a student at St. Mary's Law School in San Antonio, Texas. But really, the dream started more than three decades before that, taking root in my mind as a young boy with an entrepreneurial spirit and a drive to make money, hustle, and build something from the ground up. That dream was finally taking concrete form: I was running my own business, I had clients who trusted me, and I had a workhorse staff dedicated to making my dream a reality. I had great kids and an incredibly supportive wife.

I had the world at my fingertips.

At least, that's what was on the outside.

But concealed underneath this sweet exterior was a bitter core. Instead of celebrating on February 4, I was consumed with worry. *I thought I was going to federal prison.*

Put that on a list of phrases I never thought would come out of my mouth.

I never could have imagined I would be the subject of an FBI investigation, facing serious penalties from both the federal government and the Texas Bar. Me, a father, husband, son, brother, and lawyer. In that moment, I probably would have sold my soul to be labeled as anything but a common criminal. But there are times in our lives that radically challenge our own perceptions of ourselves. And for me, this was one of those times.

This is the story of how I ended up at one of the lowest points in my life. And how, because of that low point, I now share this story with you as a man profoundly altered, whose best-laid plans were marred by notoriety, scandal, and rejection. A story of a fall from grace so severe that it fundamentally changed who I am. And hopefully, in the end, it is a story of redemption and the healing power of community and Divine Grace.

This is the story of the Man in The Ditch. And in these pages, I am going to share that story with you.

Anyone who has ever read John Grisham will likely recognize this as the typical story arc: a rise, a fall, and a subsequent rise, bolstered (of course) by a loyal few who keep the faith while the rest of society at best walks by and at worst casts stones. But to me, it's so much more than that.

My time in The Ditch sobered me to a grim reality: *All* of us are just one left turn from The Ditch.

If we were having coffee together at Lucky's, my favorite Dallas diner, this is the part where you would do one of two things: one, grab the check and get the heck out, or two, ask: "Mike, what is this ditch thing, anyway?"

If you're still reading this book, I'm assuming you've picked option two, so here's the deal. The Ditch is a place you don't want to end up, but in some cruel twist of fate, you do. Maybe it's through your own fault. Maybe it's not. For some, The Ditch may be a scary diagnosis. A job loss. A global pandemic that changes the fabric of your family's life. Maybe it's a run-in with the law, a poor decision that spawns others and traps you in a cycle of addiction. And sometimes it's vague. Sometimes, it's just one too many hard knocks from life.

But let me make one thing clear: People in The Ditch aren't bad people. At least, not any more than the rest of us. We all have the capacity to do great good and to work great evil. In my life, I've done both. And my experience in The Ditch humbled me enough to know that no one is blameless.

That's why I'm sharing this story. Christians say that the ground is level at the foot of the Cross. I say it's also level at the bottom of The Ditch. My story involves a perfect storm of human pride and fear, involvement with the wrong people, misplaced trust, the sharp sting of betrayal, and ultimately, desperation. But it took me a long time to realize that it was a special story precisely because it was far from unique.

It takes no effort to sit at a comfortable distance and judge those who've done wrong. I've done it. But it's really, really hard to be the one to roll up your sleeves and show your scars, especially if you're donning a cloak of righteousness. It's much harder to raise your hand and admit to royally screwing up.

Throughout my life, Theodore Roosevelt's "Man in the Arena" speech has resonated with me, particularly this excerpt:

> *It is not the critic who counts; not the man who points out how the strong man stumbles, or where the doer of deeds could have done them better. The credit belongs to the man who is actually in the arena, whose face is marred by dust and sweat and blood; who strives valiantly; who errs, who comes up short again and again, because there is no effort without error and shortcoming[.]*

This image empowers me every time I share my story. And this book is my attempt to climb into Roosevelt's Arena.

I've shared my story with audiences around the country, and from that, I have come face to face with countless others who have been in The Ditch. In fact, many have dug ditches that look hauntingly similar to mine, marked by secrecy and scandal. And every time I share my story, I hear the same refrain: "Mike, now I know I'm not the only one."

By sharing my story, my hope is to encourage others with one simple fact: that they are not alone in The Ditch while everyone else sits on a mountaintop. Sharing our wounds builds bridges from ditch to ditch.

But if no one speaks up, if no one is the first to climb into The Arena, then we all lose.

Because whether you call it Original Sin, a Hobbesian Leviathan, typical dumbassery, or something else, the reality is that we are all one heartbeat, one decision, one misstep from falling into The Ditch. To give you a sense of how I went from lawyer, husband, father, and entrepreneur to the Man in The Ditch, I first need to share the stories about the people, experiences, and values that shaped me.

And if you see yourself in me, in my story, and it gives you hope?

I could ask for nothing more.

Chapter 1:
Of Hustle, Hot Dogs, and Herbie's School of Hard-Won Wisdom

Continuous effort–not strength or intelligence–is the key to unlocking our potential.

~ Winston Churchill

To understand a person–and I mean to really, truly see him–you need to know his story. But taking the time to make these leaps of empathy can be (and often continues to be) the reason it's so easy to wield the sharp sword of judgment against others. I know because I've been on both sides of the equation.

I didn't end up in The Ditch by happenstance, and so understanding my story means knowing my background: a background marked by an entrepreneurial spirit, unlikely relationships, fierce loyalty, and a hard-nosed commitment to hustle.

I was born in Chicago, the only child of a newly-single mother. My mom was forty years old when I was born (considered an advanced maternal age at that time), and ended up moving from Chicago to El Paso, Texas, to work at a phone company. But she struggled deeply with Bipolar Disorder, and raising me was a challenge.

Through her work at the phone company, she met a woman named Jean Bassett, who was married to a man named Herbie. Jean and Herbie were a light to my mother at that time, but five-year-old me never could have imagined the impact they would have on my life. When the toll of raising me under the shadow of crippling mental illness became unbearable, my mother did one of the hardest things I think a parent could ever do: She sent me to live with people she trusted even more than herself to love me in a way she felt she couldn't. I was nine years old when Herbie and Jean Bassett officially adopted me.

Growing up in Herbie and Jean's affluent community in El Paso, it would have seemed like I never had to lift a finger. My adoptive parents were well-off. Our home in the Upper Valley was just a four-minute bike ride from the El Paso Country Club, where we hobnobbed with doctors, lawyers, and others who had serious clout in our community. And Herbie and Jean were right there at the center. But they also weren't.

Herbie and Jean were unpretentious and tough as nails. And looking back, they couldn't have been more different. Jean was an artist in every sense of the word. Her pieces mixed religious iconography with the bright and bold displays familiar to Southwestern style art. She never stopped painting, and in her retirement, she turned one room of the two-bedroom condo she and Herbie shared into an art studio where my sons loved to play as they grew up.

While Jean was the "yin," Herbie was her "yang." He enlisted in the Army when he was just fourteen (lying about his age), fought throughout the entirety of World War II and the Korean War, and concluded his service as a field artillery officer. He eventually returned to El Paso and spent the rest of his working life selling insurance. And if I noticed the difference in them as a child, I can only imagine the inside jokes they shared about each other's eccentricities.

Together, Jean and Herbie were my rock, but they were also the first to knock some sense into me when I let success and popularity get to my head. Jean was kind, strong, and encouraging, and Herbie was the most stubborn man I've ever known. He was retired from the military and his life in El Paso looked quite different from his early days. To put it mildly, Herbie had a tough life. But he didn't let anyone or anything dull his resolve to be the best version of himself. He was set in his worldviews, many with which I vehemently disagreed, but he was the most egalitarian man I have ever met. Herbie taught me to treat *everyone* with dignity, from the server at the local bar to the distinguished lawyer at the country club. "You are above no one," he would tell me. He taught me that eye contact and a strong handshake had the power to bridge what seemed like impassable socioeconomic gaps, and he lived what he preached.

In the El Paso Upper Valley, many residents irrigated their lawns from massive ditches. The "ditch riders"–mostly Mexican immigrants–labored in the Texas heat, keeping an eye on the water in the ditches and irrigating the land. A man named Serafino was the ditch rider for our area. He spoke little English, and Herbie spoke no Spanish. They hailed from radically different backgrounds. But my father was the only man in the Upper Valley who would invite Serafino over for a meal. The image of the two men sharing a brown bag lunch on our lawn, breaking bread and communicating as best as they could, carved a profound and lasting image in my mind.

Still, Herbie was no softie, and for every ounce of compassion and respect he instilled in my young brain, he knocked about ten ounces of hard-earned sense. Herbie made it clear that if I wanted something, I had to earn it. So, while my friends were gifted cars and lavish vacations for high school graduation, I got one of Herbie's firm slaps on the back and a gruff, "Congratulations. You have completed the minimum education standard for the State of Texas." This is something I would half-jokingly share with my two sons decades later.

Herbie was always proud of me, but he wasn't about to give me a medal for making it through high school. His mantra was: "This life owes you nothing. If you want something, go get it." I internalized this message from a very young age. From the time I was in grade school, I always worked, and I quickly learned that I had a knack for sales. I think this may have largely been the influence of older siblings. When Herbie and Jean adopted me, I was twenty-eight years younger than their oldest child. So instead of being hazed by peers a couple of grades above my own, I had the benefit of learning about adult life from a group of people making their first earnest attempts at it.

I credit my youngest older sister, Jan, with one of my first forays into entrepreneurship. When I was young, Jan's then-husband owned a Valvoline distributorship and on occasion, he brought home corporate swag. He gave me some, and I figured out that I could make serious dough (at least by fifth-grade standards) by peddling the products to my classmates. Mesh-backed trucker hats had the highest profit margin, followed closely by mechanical pencils. A few years later, when cinnamon toothpicks were all the rage, I made my own by soaking picks in convenience-store cinnamon oil. I made a cool sixty bucks a week in 1974, until the school administration shut down my budding enterprise, explaining to Herbie and Jean that I couldn't hawk my wares on campus.

But one thing was clear: I craved financial independence. During my high school summers, I worked fifty- to sixty-hour weeks mowing lawns and selling concessions at the El Paso Diablos' baseball games. When I wanted a new stereo system for my El Camino, I bought one. If I wanted to grab beers with my buddies, I didn't have to ask for pocket money. Few things gave me more satisfaction than earning my own keep, and while I may have felt like an impostor in my privileged community, those years of hard work, entrepreneurship, and hustle made a lasting impression on me.

When I was sixteen, I landed my first "real" job at Wienerschnitzel, a West-Coast fast food institution that had made its way to Texas. The trajectory of my life changed entirely over hot dogs and grease friers. Not only did I learn how to work on a team and rise up to leadership roles, but I met my wife.

I spotted her early on, and after learning she was my good friend's sister, I got serious. "Tell me about your sister," I nagged him. He resisted as long as he could, but there was no keeping me away from Liz. To this day, she is my rock. On my last days on earth, I want to be as close to her as possible, because a giant lightning bolt will probably crash down from the heavens and smite me if she isn't near. She is a living saint, one of the strongest, most compassionate women I've ever met. What she's endured in her life would crush most people, but she's weathered it all with grace. She's as kind as the day is long, but let's face it: You can't be married to a lawyer *and* raise two sons by being a pushover.

Meeting Liz radically changed me in more ways than one, not least of all my faith. Growing up, I was what they call a "Chreester"–Christmas and Easter–Methodist. But Liz's family was and is devoutly Catholic. I learned early on that if I wanted to take her out on Saturday nights, I had to sit through the Vigil Mass first. And that's how a church-twice-a-year guy became a fixture at weekly Mass. Within a few years, we were engaged. We were married at St. Matthew's Catholic Church, just a stone's throw from my childhood home. During my second year of law school, I converted to Catholicism. My faith is, and will always be, a mainstay and a mooring for me and my family. To this day, it is one of the greatest gifts anyone has ever given me.

In 1979, I enrolled as a commuter student at the University of Texas at El Paso (fondly referred to by locals as "Harvard on the Border"), where I double-majored in accounting and management. If I studied in high school, I honestly don't recall. But at UTEP, I sure as hell did. Early on, I took a course called College Reading and Study Skills, where I learned how to make outlines, retain facts, and synthesize heaps of information, all the while enjoying the beer in the UTEP Student Union. At the time, I had no idea that these same practices would sustain me through law school, bar exam prep, and my early days as a young lawyer.

I excelled in college, and I loved it. I sailed into my senior year with a 3.9 average while still working nearly full-time at Wienerschnitzel, then eventually as a bank teller. I also enrolled in Army ROTC. With a seemingly stellar transcript, a promising career trajectory, and the love of my life at my side, I was feeling pretty great about life.

But as life tends to do, it swiftly knocked me down a few pegs.

My first dose of the realities of adult life snuck in during winter break of my Junior Year. I was spending some quality time with my oldest brother, Sterling, a Texas A&M grad, Army Ranger, and, if I'm being honest, one of the toughest, bravest men I've known. One morning, while Sterling was brushing his teeth over the bathroom sink, I chattered nonstop about everything I had seen, experienced, and accomplished at UTEP. It was clear I was feeling pretty good about myself.

Sterling spat his toothpaste in the sink, wiped his mouth, and turned to face me. "When you do something outside of 5071," he said, "come tell me."

5071 Meadowlark was our address. Our comfortable, safe, coiffed El Paso address. Sterling himself had been through Hell and back. His list of career accomplishments was longer than our grand driveway, but he uttered nary a word about them. So I was stunned, sobered, humbled, embarrassed, and frankly mad as hell when he called me on my hubristic prattling. But I needed this admonition, and it served me well. Without his tough love early on, I can only imagine my time in The Ditch would have been much worse.

Sterling suffered cruelly the last six weeks of his life, battling and ultimately succumbing to cancer. Liz and I were with him through it all. To this day, I still feel the sting of his loss. Witnessing his too-short life of quiet service left an indelible mark on me, and I will never forget his admonition: Be humble, because you never know what life is going to serve up.

Chapter 2:
The Paper Chase

The goal of education is the advancement of knowledge and the dissemination of truth.

~ John F. Kennedy

I'd known I wanted to be a lawyer since my Sophomore Year in high school. One year, at the El Paso Country Club, I met a prominent criminal defense lawyer who practiced in El Paso. I was preparing for my school's mock trial competition and he graciously offered to help me refine my cross examination. It was at that moment that I realized: *This is what I want to do with my life.* To me, it felt like getting paid to learn, to think abstractly, and to solve problems professionally. So I made up my mind: I was going to law school, and I would be a trial lawyer, just like this veteran criminal defense lawyer.

When I graduated from college, my time in the ROTC had earned me a Regular Army commission as a Second Lieutenant and I had orders to report to Hawaii, with the goal of going to Ranger School on the horizon. Just like Sterling. Still, I applied to law school at the same time, resolving to defer my military service if I got accepted and to report to Hawaii if I didn't. While I was fairly confident about my law school prospects given my college transcript, let's not forget that I was still a twenty-one-year-old college student–and college students are not universally known for their track records of solid decision making. So naturally, I decided to sit for the LSAT the day after my bachelor party.

I wasn't hung over when I reported to the testing site. I was still drunk. And let's just say there's a reason they don't let drunk people drive...or take law school admissions tests that dictate the future of their careers. Without going into too many painful details, my score left me with few choices. To give you an example of just how bleak the situation was, Stanford didn't reject me: *They sent my application money back*. Let me be perfectly clear: My application was so bleak that they didn't even want my money.

Remember Herbie's words, *this life owes you nothing*? Well, I was feeling that truth pretty profoundly at that moment.

Nonetheless, God's grace is relentless. And as luck would have it, two institutions saw something in me: I was waitlisted at Baylor University in Waco, and St. Mary's Law School in San Antonio. Liz's parents, whose friends and acquaintances in the Catholic community ran very deep, put in a good word for me with someone at the San Antonio Diocese. I don't know what was said to whom, but it must have worked. That summer, St. Mary's accepted me.

I couldn't believe it. I was going to be a lawyer.

I deferred my military service, officially enrolled, and Liz and I packed our car and headed to San Antonio. We'd never lived anywhere but El

Paso, and we knew no one. It was a lonely time, with me buried in the grim trenches of my 1L Year while Liz worked three jobs to pay the rent on our small San Antonio apartment (and by small, I mean you could vacuum the entire apartment without having to pull the plug once). But we were young and full of hope. And apparently I'd learned nothing from Sterling about humility, because I knew, just *knew*, I would crush law school.

When grades came back after the first semester, though, I learned that just the opposite was true: Law school crushed *me*. I wasn't exactly sitting pretty at number 230 out of about 300 total students, and all I could think as I incredulously turned that grade postcard over and over in my hands was, *well...shit*.

But Herbie's "life owes you nothing, Michael" mantra, coupled with the hustle that had come to define me from such a young age, took over, and I set to work. I knew I needed to step up my game and relearn what I thought I knew. I hearkened back to my College Reading and Study Skills class and rewired my brain to tackle law school exams. Three years of long nights and grueling study sessions later, it paid off. I graduated in 1987, number twelve in my class of 206. (That's right. 206 out of the roughly 300 that started. An attrition rate of about thirty percent was normal for St. Mary's Law School at that time. So, simply being a part of the cohort that survived was a victory in and of itself.)

I loved the people I met at St. Mary's, but hated law school itself. Poring over massive tomes of antiquated case law made my eyes glaze over, but to fulfill my dream of becoming a lawyer, I knew I had to buckle down and do the work. I treated it like a job and learned that while I was not the smartest in my class, I could outwork almost anyone. I had never seen my nose so close to the grindstone, but in time, I realized I just had to do one simple thing: Show up every single damn day and do the simple, unglamorous work.

Liz and I welcomed our first son, C.J., in the middle of finals in my last year of law school. I remember studying for my property exam in the hospital library. When I reported for the exam, a wave of exhaustion overtook me. *I'll just put my head down for one minute,* I told myself. After all, I had three hours to take the test. In what seemed like mere seconds, I looked up and saw that my "one minute" had become several hours. There were only four minutes left, with much more than four minutes of exam material to pour through.

The professor gave me a C–proof that God really does exist–and I walked the graduation stage a few months later: a new father, and a new lawyer.

Chapter 3:
Becoming The Bassett Firm

The true test of the American ideal is whether we're able to recognize our failings and then rise together to meet the challenges of our time. Whether we allow ourselves to be shaped by events and history, or whether we act to shape them. Whether chance of birth or circumstance decides life's big winners and losers, or whether we build a community where, at the very least, everyone has a chance to work hard, get ahead, and reach their dreams.

~ Barack Obama

After law school, I landed a coveted position as a Briefing Attorney at the Texas Supreme Court in Austin. When I got the call, I flew into our little apartment to break the news to Liz. I had a job! I was employed! I was a real lawyer! Liz looked at me, smiled, and quipped: "That's great. Now you need to take the trash out."

We moved to Austin in the summer of 1987, and so began one of the best years of my young adult life. Liz and I had our second son, Kyle, in the Summer of 1988. I made a paltry Briefing Attorney salary, but I loved every minute of my job. I met some of the smartest people on the Court and witnessed a very interesting year in Texas politics. I watched Mike Wallace setting up in the conference room for interviews, shared daily coffee with my Judge, and authored judicial opinions. But I also learned that in government work, you can only do what you can do: When the assignments are done, so too is the workday. So when I finished my weekly work early, I played ping pong in the basement at the Court. My ping-pong game was top-notch that year.

Liz and I loved Austin and leaned into our lives as new professionals. When my clerkship ended, I took a job with Cowles and Thompson, one of the top civil defense firms in Texas. I was lucky enough to gain incredible trial experience and work with brilliant lawyers. Chuck Green was my direct supervisor and a wise mentor. He taught me so much about being a lawyer, and I owe much of who I am today to his guidance. Not only did he drag me out of defending medical-malpractice cases, he introduced me to trucking work (a massive component of my current practice). He also taught me early on what mattered most. "It's not hard," he would tell me. "You just have to know what to do. It's *persistent* work. But it's not *hard.*" The analogy he used was simple. Imagine you are driving from coast to coast seeking the best diners in every state. You have two options: 1) Start driving east, or 2) use a map and follow directions. As Chuck would say, it's not difficult to know which option is better. Implementing the plan faithfully is where the rubber meets the road...and where the strong separate themselves from those who are too daunted by the journey to see it through.

Chuck also instilled in me some of the values that drive my Firm today, mainly, cultivating a practice that is others-centered. As a young lawyer, I slowly learned that the law is not about me or my own ambitions.

It is about the clients. Every. Single. Time. Some of the principles Chuck taught me have become mainstays of my practice: Make the people you serve, whether clients or colleagues, feel like they are the only ones. Listen seventy-five percent of the time and talk twenty-five percent of it. Ask them what they need, and they will tell you. And most importantly, show up every single day and faithfully do the day's simple, persistent work.

Chuck's lessons sunk into my bones, but my time at Cowles taught me another valuable lesson: I stole a glimpse into the business of law. I slowly started to learn how a law firm runs, how to market, how to bill, and how to keep the pipeline full of work. This lit a fire under me. I loved the law as a distinguished profession, but I loved the hustle even more. I knew I couldn't stray far from my entrepreneurial roots, and it didn't take long for me to learn that I just wasn't wired for big firm life.

Four years into my time at Cowles, I was doing quite well, billing more than 200 hours a month. But I also had a young family, and my goal was to leave by 5:30 p.m. every day so I could have dinner with them. This meant I generally headed to the office before the sun rose, long before the rest of the team showed up (lawyers are notoriously *not* morning people). And to make matters worse, in the late 1980s, big firms were hopelessly tied to the fiction that "you never leave before the boss," leaving hordes of young lawyers chained to their desks for twelve, fourteen, or even sixteen hours a day.

One day, a young partner took note of my early departure time and castigated me for it. "We need to know you are committed," he told me. "You need to keep up your hours, and there's no way you're doing that if you're leaving so early." I replied by telling him I'd make him a deal. "You get your happy ass here when I do," I said, "and I'll stay as late as you stay." I never said discretion was my strong suit–especially at the ripe age of twenty-eight.

Thankfully, I never had to hold up my end of the deal, because I left the firm in 1992 to join a startup firm made up of Cowles alumni. I worked my way up to partner and from there, laid the foundation that would eventually become The Bassett Firm.

Today, I run my very own law practice on the principles that shaped me. Herbie's egalitarianism and respect for all people. His understanding that life owes us nothing, and if we want something, we need to do the work. Sterling's quiet, strong humility. His recognition that you can't just walk back into the office and take a victory lap while the coffee is still warm. And, of course, Liz's tough love and abiding kindness and loyalty, her uncanny ability to be a tangible and emotional anchor when it seems all is adrift.

This is all baked into our work environment at The Bassett Firm. I still show up at dawn and generally leave before dusk to eat dinner at home. That's what works for me, and I've always tried to encourage our lawyers to do their work during the hours that they function best. I expect a lot from them, and they deliver in spades. We are a self-reported dysfunctional family. We share breakfast together on Fridays, swap stories, and tease one another mercilessly. At times, we stay at the office far too late working through case strategy, or simply picking up the pieces of that day's challenges, bit by bit, always together. But I know this drive comes from a singular agreement: Our practice is dedicated, heart and soul, to the very person we exist to serve in the first place:

The Man in The Ditch.

I wish I could take credit for this touchstone, but the attribution goes to one of my original team-members, Staci Cassidy. The daughter of a Lutheran minister, she was the first to draw the parallel between our work and the Parable of the Good Samaritan. And because of this, she helped me realize that at any given time, about a third of our team finds themselves in The Ditch. A diagnosis. A job loss. A financial crisis. And as a leader in constant training, my job is to meet them there, in the muck and mire, at the bottom of The Ditch. Because if we can't take care of each other, we can't nurture those who are in our care: clients, colleagues, family. And if we can't take care of them, we can't fulfill our duties as lawyers and counselors at law.

So much of what we do is listening, guiding, and sharing compassion— to be a North Star in troubling times. Not to sit back comfortably, judge those in The Ditch, and opt to serve only those who stand on high ground. Our job is to throw down a ladder and climb in with them.

And if there is one thing I've learned in my life, it's that there are two types of people: those who will climb down into The Ditch with you, and those who won't. You need to know one from the other.

Chapter 4:
Into The Ditch

"The dark does not destroy the light; it defines it. It's our fear of the dark that casts our joy into the shadows."

~ Brené Brown

Young lawyers quickly learn that it takes some time to figure out what type of work they love and hate, and I was no exception. When I was still a newly-minted associate at Cowles and Thompson, it didn't take long for me to realize that medical malpractice was not my cup of tea. Thank God for Chuck Green, who introduced me to my legal lifeblood: representing trucking companies and truck drivers.

The first time Chuck introduced me to one of our commercial trucking clients, I remember saying to myself: "These are my people." Hard-working, no-nonsense early-risers, these folks felt like kindred spirits. Not to mention, the work was interesting and abundant. We represented large trucking companies when a driver was involved in a highway accident. It was a passion as much as a number's game: If American truckers collectively traverse over 140 billion miles per year, something is bound to go awry.

It was inevitable, then, that when I moved on from Cowles in 1992, I wouldn't be able to stay away from trucking work for long. Shortly after I joined a group of lawyers that had broken off from Cowles, I got a call from a claims professional assigning me a new truck wreck case. Given that I was the "new guy" at this firm, I was happy to get the assignment and hopefully be known as someone who could bring in business. So I gave the adjuster a wholehearted *yes*. Trucking cases were our gateway into a whole new world of profitable business for my firm.

And so began my relationship with Sam.

Sam was the Director of Risk Management for a holding company that had multiple trucking companies under its umbrella. The holding company was massive and its subsidiary trucking companies had *lots* of trucks on the road, all over the United States. Sam managed the litigation that flowed from all of these companies. One of these subsidiary trucking companies was involved in this new lawsuit. Working for Sam–and doing good work for him–set off a firestorm of business for our small firm. Because of this, Sam quickly became a fixture in our practice *and* in my life.

Sam was Italian, and his personality reflected his heritage. He was a big guy with a big personality, loud and gregarious, who loved food, wine, and swapping stories around the table. Truly magnetic personalities are rare, and Sam was one of them. From the moment I met him, he made me feel like we were best buds, like I was a part of his tribe. And being part of Sam's tribe was a very, very good thing for any lawyer. Sam was a king maker: He knew how to connect people to opportunities, and opportunities to big money. And while I never knew whether he, himself, was well-off, he certainly knew how to keep others busy, including me.

This is not just because Sam was a force to be reckoned with, but because he was damn good at his job. He knew the trucking industry inside and out and could spot risk from a mile away. He was the ideal client. He was supremely low maintenance, smart, and engaged, and he never needed hand-holding. And did I mention he paid his bills within thirty days?

Sam and I enjoyed a mutually beneficial relationship for years. He sent us new trucking cases and connected us to some of the biggest players in the industry while we worked hard on his cases and, as much as possible, invited him to indulge in some of the perks of the job.

Every person is complex, and Sam brought his own vices to the table. While Sam was low-maintenance when it came to case logistics, he was very into some of these perks one would expect from early 1990s business culture. Sam loved to travel, to be wined and dined, and to have a good time (sometimes maybe a bit *too* good). I'd take him to dinner after a deposition or mediation, and often as we parted ways, he would announce that he had different plans for the rest of the evening. I always declined to join, but Sam never failed to regale me with stories of his escapades.

But Sam and I also developed what I saw as a deeper connection, beyond just the attorney-and-client who bonded over dinner a few times a year. Sam attended Mass with my family and visited our home to break bread with me, Liz, and the boys. In fact, he was one of the *very* few clients who has ever set foot inside my house. Our dinners would last hours, punctuated by laughter and stories. That's just the kind of guy Sam was. He made friends everywhere he went. And when you have dinner with someone eight to ten times a year and that person is physically present for every milestone in some of the major cases you handle, you can't help but start to feel a unique bond.

It doesn't seem far-fetched, then, to admit that I *thought* Sam and I were pretty tight. I *thought* this was one of those great deals where you can be friends with your client. After all, isn't that what we all want? As a lawyer, you are going to make withdrawals from the emotional bank account in any client relationship. I did that with Sam. I just didn't know what it would cost me.

In 1996, another lawyer and I split off from our firm and started our own law practice with four lawyers, two paralegals, and three secretaries. We were scared to death but hung our shingle anyway. In just five years, we had grown to more than fifteen lawyers and a total staff of over thirty. Business was great. "When someone gives you an entire stable, you don't waste time looking a gift horse in the mouth," as Herbie would say.

In February of 2001, about nine years after I first met Sam, I walked into my office to see a massive package sitting on the floor by my office door. It was from Sam. This certainly wasn't out of the ordinary. Sam was known to send his attorneys lavish gifts, so I smiled to myself as I tore it open and started digging out the contents. I was not surprised Sam sent such gifts, but in this moment, my eyes popped out of my head: That box contained some *serious* swag.

Super Bowl season was approaching, and Sam, always plugged into the football scene, had milked all the right people for my benefit. Inside the package was a wealth of football paraphernalia that would make my two sons giddy with excitement: signed footballs, jerseys, and impressive, life-like watercolor paintings of the Packers. I couldn't believe how generous it was–but then again, I could. Everything about Sam was over the top, and his gifts were no exception.

But when I called him to thank him, his response was strange.

"Did you get everything out of the box?" he asked.

I paused. There was a lot in the box, but I said that yes, I had seen it all: the footballs, the jerseys, the artwork. He replied by asking me to dig through the contents to make sure I'd found the envelopes at the bottom. I checked, and sure enough, I saw two envelopes at the bottom of the box. I tore them open, then froze.

"I'll need to call you back," I told him, then hung up.

The envelopes held a series of checks totaling about $10,000. They were made out to me, not the Firm, which was strange. I then noticed that the reference line on each check listed a different case name. I recognized the names of the trucking companies enough to know that these were companies Sam managed. But the problem was, none of the checks pertained to a case I was handling for Sam.

Assuming this was an honest mistake, and dismissing the oddity of receiving payment this way (my clients typically didn't bury their checks in giant boxes of Super Bowl swag), I called Sam back with every intention of setting the record straight.

"Sam, these aren't my cases. I think you meant to send these to someone else," I said.

"Not a mistake," Sam replied tersely. "Cash them."

What?

I repeated myself, telling him that no, he didn't understand. These were meant for someone else. He'd made a mistake. But Sam shot right back:

"Cash them. Run the money through your trust account. Then we'll split it."

I suddenly lost my ability to formulate words. *What was happening? Was he really asking me to do what I thought? There was no way. I trusted Sam. We were friends. He was...Sam. There was no way he'd ask me to do something so shady. I had to be missing something.*

"Sam?" I asked, tentatively, knowing all too well that personal finance can be a delicate subject, "do you need money? I would be more than happy to lend you the $10,000." But Sam cut me off, his tone hardening in a way I'd never heard before.

"Cash them."

His change in tone was making me nervous and I started to feel clammy. All I wanted was to clear this up, to get off the phone and get on with my day. So before I could stop myself, I burst out:

"No. I can't do that."

If you've ever watched the famous cross-examination scene from *A Few Good Men*, you've got a good frame of reference for how dramatically this conversation turned. If Sam's tone had shifted slightly before, then my refusal brought out an entirely different persona. It was as though the person on the other end of the phone was not my friend and colleague of more than nine years, but an aggressive, nasty character the likes of which I'd never known.

"*Do it,*" he said. "And if you don't, I'm pulling all my business from you and telling everyone in the industry that you've lost your shit."

Click.

I sat there in my empty office, the dial tone on the dead call sounding like a flat-lined electrocardiogram, football swag strewn across my desk, and those awful, bogus checks hanging limply in my hands. A string of four-letter words swirled through my head and blocked out any semblance of rational thought. This was so out of left-field that it couldn't have been real. Yes, I knew Sam had his vices. He loved wine and women a bit too much, but he was not a criminal. He would never actually blackmail someone, especially not one of his close friends. We'd been in some high-pressure situations together, and I'd never seen him come apart like this. I didn't think he had it in him.

But when I finally had a chance to piece together what had just happened, I (wrongly) convinced myself that I was stuck in some nightmarish zero-sum game. I could either cash the checks, risking not only criminal liability but also my livelihood, or face losing what I remember being about $500,000 in annual revenue to our firm. In other words, if I didn't do what Sam demanded, half a million dollars in business would walk out the door and the professional reputation I worked so hard to build would be torched. But if I cashed the checks, who knew what type of nefarious business I'd be involving myself in. I'd be tainted and dirty, just like those checks.

At the time, it never occurred to me that there was a third option: to call Sam's boss to tell him that Sam was embezzling from him. It also never occurred to me that I couldn't have been the only one who'd received a nice, big "let's commit fraud together" swag box from Sam. His connections in the industry ran so deep and thick that there was no way he hadn't already attempted to strongarm someone else. Maybe even *many* others.

But at that point, I wasn't thinking like a rational thirty-nine-year-old lawyer. I was viewing the world in the construct Sam had set up for me, a false dichotomy that involved two equally destructive choices: either win Sam's approval–and his business–by participating in something slimy, or resolve to do the "right" thing and risk losing more than half of my business. In my mind, there was no gray area, no middle ground. And I think that is because at that moment, I was suddenly six years old again, shuffled between my birth mother's home and Jean and Herbie's house in El Paso.

I was the kid who didn't really know where he belonged–and if, in fact, he belonged *anywhere*. All I knew was that I didn't want to be alone, to be abandoned, cast-off. And from childhood, I had this message stamped on my heart: *If I make someone angry, I will be abandoned.* At that time, I wasn't aware of just how much that message had been ingrained in me, of how much that six-year-old was still driving my decisions.

Now I was facing abandonment yet again, but this time, by a friend. A friend who also happened to help sustain my business. Business in an industry where I was liked and respected. Where people knew me. Where I worked extremely hard to build a solid reputation. I couldn't have that taken from me. I couldn't have Sam telling everyone I'd lost it, because then, I wouldn't just be abandoned by Sam. I would be abandoned by everyone. And who would I be if that happened?

So I cashed the checks.

I can still feel my heart slamming against my ribs as I signed the back of each check and presented them to the bank teller. I just knew, deep down, that everyone knew what I was up to, knew that I was involved in something really, really wrong. But I'd made my decision. I got the money and put it all in an envelope.

A few days later, I was wheels-up to Las Vegas, Sam's money tucked into my carry-on bag. Every year, I traveled there with a group of friends to blow off some steam for a few days, and Sam, not one to miss out on a good time, caught wind of our annual shenanigans and invited himself along. At some point on that trip, in the lobby of the MGM Grand, I pulled Sam aside and slipped him the envelope, in just the same shady, secretive fashion in which he'd hidden those checks at the bottom of my swag box.

"Never do this to me again," I said.

He never did. And we never spoke of it.

Because that's what one does with secrets. You bury them.

Chapter 5:
The Operation of Grace

Having faith does not mean having no difficulties, but having the strength to face them, knowing we are not alone.

~ Pope Francis

Almost a year passed and no one was the wiser. But the weight of my secret wasn't lost on me. I lived on pins and needles, waiting to be found out. It felt like waiting for a cancer diagnosis that you just knew was coming, even before the doctor called you with the test results. It was absolute agony.

In retrospect, I knew Sam had groomed me. I knew other lawyers who worked with Sam, and he never did this to them. While I thought we were building a solid friendship, he was testing the waters. And looking back, he must have been pretty good at it. He must have never tested anyone who said no and refused to do his bidding, because that would have stopped him in his tracks. But for all the years he had been building a relationship with me, he had just been priming the pump.

When the time came to put *me* to the test, Sam knew I'd fall for it. And I did.

On January 16, 2002, nearly a year after Sam sent me the swag box, I got a call at my office. It was Sam. He told me that after months of internal audits with his employer, the FBI had picked up his case. They were on to him. On to *us*. At this point, I knew it was over. I hung up the phone and left the office without saying anything to anyone. It was 8:30 in the morning.

As I drove my pickup down the familiar path toward home, my heart sunk more and more. I knew I had to tell Liz, though there was never anything I'd wanted to do less. And to make matters worse, because we'd decided to raise our family outside of Dallas, I had almost an hour in morning traffic to marinate over the horrors that were unfolding. I remember thinking that all I had to do was cross the freeway and run headlong into an eighteen-wheeler, and that conversation wouldn't have to happen. It terrifies me to think just how tempting that option was. And how close I came to doing it.

I pulled into our driveway to find carefree, lighthearted commotion at the house. We were renovating our kitchen, and the guys had already arrived to start their daily work. Liz, who was at home overseeing the work, saw my car and came out to greet me. She looked innocently surprised to see me home on a Tuesday morning, and the mere sight of her made me unravel at the seams. I started sobbing–a grown man in his suit and tie, standing in his driveway at 9:30 AM on a weekday, losing his shit.

To casual passersby, I looked like a loser. But to me, I looked much worse than that. I had officially become The Man in the Ditch.

"I'm so sorry," was all I could say, over and over and over. "I'm so sorry. I'm so sorry. I've ruined it for all of us."

It took me a very long time to compose myself enough to tell Liz the story. I don't know if we were outside or inside. I don't remember what she said or how she reacted. I don't remember the hammering and drilling going on in our kitchen or whether anyone else saw or heard. All I know is that day was worse than the days I lost my parents, my brother, and my sister, combined. Admitting not only my foolishness and duplicity, but also the fact that I'd carried it around for a year in secret, eviscerated me.

I vaguely remember Liz pushing me to call a lawyer. As a lawyer myself, that should've been my first thought. But then again, there's not much room for rational thought at the bottom of The Ditch. So with her encouragement, I dialed Martin LeNoir, a criminal defense attorney who represented our truckers in associated criminal matters. I told him we needed to talk, and he agreed to see me that day.

I was in no condition to drive, so Liz drove us to Martin's office. The entire way there, she kept squeezing my hand and repeating, over and over, *"it will be ok. It will be ok."* I was not in a position to appreciate the grace she was showing me at that time, but her loyalty and faithfulness are not lost on me now. I remember very little from our meeting with Martin, but I do recall telling him, as I'd said to Liz, that it was all over. *I'm done,* I said. *I'm not going to practice law anymore. They are going to lock me up.* But Martin did what a lawyer should do–and what I utterly failed to do in that moment: He chose to think like a lawyer.

"Bullshit." He deadpanned, staring me straight in the eyes. I sat up straighter. *What?*

"You were extorted," Martin said. "This motherfucker has probably done this same thing to other people. What a sorry piece of shit he is."

I wish I could tell you I believed Martin, but I was still not thinking clearly. I was still convinced I was the worst thing to ever crawl into his office. Although it took years to sink in, in retrospect, I think that his words gave me a semblance of what might have been hope, the first small stirrings of a realization that I was less of a criminal and more of a man who had simply gotten in bed with the wrong person and made a very real, very human mistake.

After walking us through what to expect from the storm clouds on the horizon, Martin referred me to a psychiatrist and suggested I see him that day. I'm glad he did, because I think the only thing more startling than the legal mess I'd gotten myself into was my anguished mental state. Liz shuffled my sad, defeated self to our car once again. We stopped for lunch at Chili's, which must've been quite a sight–me with my red eyes and shaking hands, Liz trying to console me, a sad pair slouched into those plastic booths over greasy food. We paid for the food, which I'd hardly touched, then headed to my appointment.

The psychiatrist was an ancient gentleman, so utterly unperturbed by my situation that I thought I was living in some alternate reality. Once I spilled my story, he looked at me thoughtfully for a moment. "You made a mistake," he admitted, "but let's be honest here. You didn't chop your family up and feed them to the dogs," he said. "So, calm down, take your meds, and come back and see me."

When we arrived home that night, I was beyond numb from the day's events: that is, until my phone started blowing up. Imagine you're still reeling from the most shameful day of your life, then thirty-eight of your colleagues call you to ask why you walked out on your work and if something fishy is going on. For the next year and a half, *every time* my phone rang, my heart would drop to the depths of my stomach and I'd feel ill.

When I sunk onto the couch after fielding a barrage of phone calls from curious colleagues, I told Liz, once again, that I was done. My law license would be stripped, I would probably go to prison, and my family would live with the stain of my disgrace for the rest of their lives. Then Liz, who finally exhausted all of her patience, cut me off.

"No." she said. "You're *not* done. This is a speed bump, sure. But you are meant to be a lawyer. So you know what? That's what you're going to be. You are going to keep practicing law, and you're going to start tomorrow."

It was not warm encouragement. It was not fluffy reassurance. It was a bold, firm, calm, and confident admonition. Liz was calling me to a higher place. Out of The Ditch, and back onto the path I'd been steadily trodding until this cyclone of bad decision making led me astray. She wasn't wasting time mincing words, mending my wounds. She was climbing down into The Ditch, grabbing me firmly by the hand, and yanking with all of her might (admittedly, after maybe one or two figurative, sobering slaps in the face).

Talking to Liz was one challenge, but sharing my downfall with my sons was another one entirely. At the time, our oldest, C.J., was fifteen and Kyle was fourteen. We held a family conference to share what had just happened, and their reactions revealed maturity and grace beyond their years. The incredible thing about kids is that when their parents tell them it will all work out, they take it as truth and hang onto it.

They were no exception, and if they were ever angry with me, they never showed it.

And I *know* that they were angry with me. How could they not be? I had turned the entire family upside down. Liz and I had been very intentional about eliminating unnecessary drama and chaos in our family. And with one stupid decision, I had thrown a wrench into the machine and the gears ground to a halt.

There is a whole part of this incident that they have yet to unpack, even two decades later. At the time, all of us compartmentalized our lives as best as we could, and there was a great deal of my fall from grace that we all deliberately chose not to discuss. Call it survival. Call it what you want. I am not proud of it and I wish it was different. But that hasn't stopped them from being my biggest cheerleaders.

They didn't just rally around me: They rallied around each other. C.J. protected, and continues to protect, Kyle in ways I think he's still unpacking. And because of that protection, Kyle was able to become the writer in the family and his fingerprints are all over the keynote speech that led to this book. I'll never forget the first time I shared this story publicly in November of 2019. Both boys attended with Liz and I kept stealing glances at them: three points of light at the back of the ballroom, holding hands. And each time l looked up, I felt a swell of gratitude for my tribe. The O.G. Bassetts.

I know that season was hard for my sons. High school already poses its social challenges, but high school in a very small town only ups the ante. And having a dad who was looking at federal prison time didn't exactly help them ascend to the highest echelons of small town Texas adolescent society. But the incredible thing about our tribe is that nonetheless, my time in The Ditch made us all a much stronger family.

I believe strongly in what we Catholics call the Operation of Grace. God's will is not to be obstructed, and I think that He is dogged in his pursuit of us. Like Liz, He wasn't about to let me call it quits on the path He'd prepared for me. So as Grace and luck would have it, a man named Jim Stanton reached out to me the very next day. Jim was a local lawyer and though we'd had a few cases together, I didn't know him well. So when he suggested we meet at the Starbucks at 75 and Mockingbird, I figured I had nothing to lose. After all, he didn't call me to shame me, point fingers, or make me feel an inch tall as so many other lawyers had...and that was something.

I remember it was bitter cold that day, and I showed up in a black leather jacket. Stanton shot me an appraising look before blurting out: "Wow! You look like SHIT." (He was never one to tiptoe around feelings.) We talked for hours over bold, black coffees, and while I can't recall the details, I do remember Jim offering, for no apparent reason, to let me use his office if I wanted to hang my shingle. I have no idea what motivated him to help me or how his offer merged so seamlessly with Liz's insistence that I was meant to keep practicing law. So by some miraculous marriage of divine intervention and newfound motivation, I spent the next two weeks setting up my very own law firm in the conference room at Stanton's Dallas office.

At this point, all of my belongings were still at my old firm, and I hadn't been there since the day I walked out without speaking to anyone. My relationship with my law partner had been, let's just say, rocky since then—he filed a Bar grievance against me—and so I was not particularly in the mood to waltz into the office to collect my files. We hired movers to pick them up, and when the folders and boxes arrived at Stanton's office, I realized someone had clearly rifled through them. It had to be the FBI. The thought that federal investigators had searched my belongings nauseated me and sent weird chills up and down my spine. But with the help of a few faithful alumni from my old firm, who inexplicably jumped ship to join our ragtag team, I rolled up my sleeves, shook the dust off my feet, and started reorganizing my files.

I remember little from those early days, as the pain of being "found out" still sliced through me. The disgrace sat heavily on my heart, and the constant, nagging fear of being sent to prison filled me with an almost constant sense of dread. But I do remember snapshots: my files taking up more than half of Stanton's narrow office hallway, the few clients who called me to tell me they were still "in," and the loyal staff who popped over from the old office to join me.

I'll never forget when Staci Cassidy, that stellar young associate, showed up one day at Stanton's office. She told me that she'd heard a lot of unbecoming chatter about me, but that her Lutheran pastor father (who has since become my dear friend) encouraged her to go with her gut.

"He asked me who I trust," she told me, "and I said 'I trust Mike.' And he told me, 'then that's who you need to follow.'"

I was beyond humbled, but there was also a part of me that thought, *"you're a damn fool, Mike."*

I also remember a paralegal at my old firm gave me the benefit of the doubt and joined us, too. Then Liz declared herself our bookkeeper, and with that, The Bassett Firm was born: a collection of people who trusted me, trusted the process, and took a serious risk in spite of themselves.

To say I felt unworthy was a massive understatement. There was no positive self-talk running through my head. That channel was dead. No signal whatsoever. It was only because of the people who rallied around me that I continued to put one foot in front of the other. It wasn't so much what they said, but what they did, that made me realize I could move forward.

That's the power of loyalty. It's knowing that someone has royally screwed something up and choosing to say, you know what, I trust this guy, and I'm going with him anyway.

The power of loyalty, and the Operation of Grace.

Chapter 6:
The Crucible

This world of ours...must avoid becoming a community of dreadful fear and hate, and be, instead, a proud confederation of mutual trust and respect.

~ Dwight D. Eisenhower

The Bassett Firm was Mike 2.0: my redemption story, my ticket out of The Ditch and back into the practice of law and, eventually, public favor. Nothing had come back to roost with the Sam situation yet–I still had my Texas Bar license and the FBI had not contacted me–so I threw everything I had into my work to distract myself. In those early days, Liz, Staci, a few loyal staff members, and I spent our days grinding around Stanton's conference table. It was rough and scrappy work, but the memories are strangely sweet. I still have the notebook Liz used to write our business plan, and the memories and images of us hunched over laptops in that tiny conference room make me smile.

Within a week of my flame-out, I went to our local bank and asked for a line of credit to finance the Firm. As though I deserved another miracle, we got one. I couldn't believe our luck. With our new funding, a small team, office space, and a few faithful clients, we started to grow.

Frankly, the only reason The Bassett Firm opened in the first place was Liz. But for her insistence that I was meant to be a lawyer, I don't think I ever would have done it. She was never one for pep talks. Rather, her admonition to me was a calm, confident voice saying: *This is what you were meant to do.* Sometimes, that is all we need. Not a saccharine reassurance that the sun is going to come out and we will all sing "Imagine" and sway by a campfire together, but just a strong, assuring voice slicing through the darkness to speak Truth. The defining moment is the space between our trials and the decision we make to either turn away, or to listen.

In those early days, my work was my therapy, and in some ways, it was much better than the meds that my psychiatrist prescribed. I think this is because when your mind is focused on solving pressing, time-sensitive issues–which is the nature of litigation–your mind leaves little room for negative self talk and anxiety to fester. So I threw myself into my work, and it helped.

But those days weren't easy.

First of all, between hiring Martin to represent me on the criminal side, and eventually, a lawyer named Jim Burnham to handle the Texas Bar grievance filed against me, I wrote a total of $150,000 in checks for lawyers in just one week. (You see, I'm accustomed to being the one *receiving* the checks for legal fees, not writing them.) Sticker shock aside, every single day required a Herculean effort to just put one foot in front of the other.

Granted, opening my Firm was nothing short of a miracle, from amassing a loyal team to scoring office space and a line of credit. But nothing was resolved with the Sam situation. I had no contact with him or the FBI, but my impending plea hearing with the Federal Government and subsequent Bar grievance hearing hung over my exposed neck like the Sword of Damocles.

I'd taken a plea deal, and my sentencing hearing was in August, 2002, in a federal courthouse in Milwaukee (Sam's company was located in Wisconsin). I remember very little of it, except that it felt like the courtroom was roughly the size of a basketball court and the Judge sat about three stories above me. I think that our minds have a way of blurring out the most traumatic events in our lives, but I distinctly remember the Judge's words when he imparted my sentence: a sentence that, miraculously, involved no prison time, but ninety days in a federal prison halfway house.

"You made a terrible mistake," he told me, "but don't let that mistake define you."

I sensed that the Judge saw something in me and believed I would get through that dark time. And somehow, his encouragement made me believe it just a little, too. After all, if you know anything about federal judges, "warm and fuzzy" isn't exactly the first image they conjure.

My Bar grievance hearing was held that November in Dallas, ironically, at a location right across the street from my old law firm. And while the federal courtroom felt like a king's chamber shrouded in mystique and glory, the Bar hearing took place in a crappy conference room with a cheap table that realistically sat six (seven would be stretching it) but which absolutely strained to accommodate ten. Aside from Jim Burnham, my old law partner was there, along with the General Counsel of the trucking companies Sam managed *and* the full Texas Bar Grievance Committee. It was like sitting in a room with your spurned lover, or perhaps a hitman gunning for his pound of flesh. It was clear I was not only dead to my old law partner but also a *persona non grata* in the transportation industry. Frankly, though, all I wanted in that moment was to get the hell out of that stale little room.

Those who have never been in The Ditch often have a hard time understanding that no one is more disgusted by the situation than the very person who landed himself there. And for those few excruciating hours, I sat silently while a group of people I'd once admired took turns rubbing my nose in my plight. It wasn't a conversation: It was a brutal acknowledgement of my screw-up. And I'd be lying if I said I didn't think some of them enjoyed it.

Once again, though, I witnessed the power of Grace and mercy: I walked away with a public reprimand, my Texas Bar license intact. That was it. The only thing that would've been better would have been a private reprimand, but beggars can't be choosers, and at that point, I knew I was back in the hunt. Until the grievance hearing, my only thought was, *is this plane going down?* But once I got through it, I felt instant relief, coupled with the sobering reality that the road ahead was still long and dark. I was reeling from the trauma of what happened with Sam, filled with a toxic mixture of self-loathing and wounded pride as I watched hordes of clients and lawyers turn their backs on me, and aching from the burden of carrying my secret for a year. I turned to drinking to numb the pain. Back then, our county was still "dry," which left a man with few options other than swinging by a convenience store on the way home from the office. The number of times I poured a forty-ounce beer into a Big Gulp cup just to make it through the loneliness of the drive home is one I'm thankful I can't count.

In those days, every step I took toward redemption felt laborious and painful. That season was penitential, like a heavy wool coat you put on in the dead of a Texas summer. It turned out that a lot of people took pleasure in my plight, especially when the Bar released the news of my reprimand. This is human nature, though: to revel in seeing the mighty fall. Not that I am saying I was mighty before, but people do love to hate lawyers, and that celebration of my reprobation sent me down a whole new shame spiral.

For a few months, I was radioactive. I remember an incensed phone call from a lawyer who'd previously given me a stellar reference, believing I'd duped her into lying about my character. At best, people who previously called me to leverage my connections in the industry simply acted like they didn't know me. At worst, they actively tore me down.

It hurt, but while I realized I could be angry, I chose instead to take a lesson from the Jesuits: When someone hurts you, the best thing you can do is to live your life in such a way that you never become that kind of person. Since then, I've chosen to stand by people who've messed up. And in this broken world of ours, I've had plenty of opportunities to do just that.

Because everyone–every single soul that graces this earth–carries a duffle-bag-sized load of shit. And frankly, that's how I like my people: real, flawed, and trodding a constant path to refinement and growth. The ones who are happy and plastic and have no faults? Those people scare me. But then again, not everyone has had the privilege of being in The Ditch.

To this day, I hold The Ditch in two places. It was the greatest trial of my life, but also an invitation to the deepest, most authentic gratitude I've ever felt. For me, The Ditch was a crucible. Without it, I would have been stuck at the emotional age of thirty-nine. In order to see tremendous growth, I also had to fail. I had to weather tremendous suffering in order to be redeemed. I think that you have to be broken down before you can be built back up. It is a physiological fact. When you work out, you need to break down your muscles so that they can repair themselves and get stronger. It is the same case spiritually, psychologically, and emotionally: Suffering is the singular path to true learning and growth.

It is the only way.

Chapter 7:
The (Long and Painful) Road to Redemption

"Everything can be taken from a man but one thing: the last of the human freedoms—to choose one's attitude in any given set of circumstances, to choose one's own way."

~ *Viktor Frankl*, **Man's Search for Meaning**

When you've been in The Ditch and you're clear-eyed about how you got there, it's impossible not to show mercy to others. Thomas Aquinas once wrote: "The old and the wise who consider that they may fall on evil times...are more inclined to mercy." I was the recipient of mercy from so many, from Liz and Jim Stanton, to Staci, to the clients who stuck with me, the bankers who gave me credit to run our Firm, to the Bar Grievance Committee who chose to issue a public reprimand instead of yanking my license. These people offered grace, mercy, and forgiveness when I couldn't find it in myself. But once I was filled up with it, I felt free to dole it out to others:

first, to myself, and then, to Sam.

About a year after launching The Bassett Firm, Martin LeNoir called me to let me know Sam was going to prison. It turned out that indeed, I was far from the only one he'd extorted. He embezzled a collective million-plus dollars from lawyers and firms that represented his companies, and trucking lawyers across the country were going down. In fact, one lawyer had cashed over $250,000 in illicit checks. This made my $10,000 feel like chump change, and it chilled me to think of the burden that lawyer was probably carrying.

At that point, maybe I should've felt relieved. Vindicated. Comforted in knowing I wasn't Sam's only target. But somehow, it only inflamed my anger. All I could think was, "I got played." And oddly enough, I couldn't bring myself to find anger toward Sam: only myself. Instead of thinking, *how dare he?* or, *how could he have done this to me?* the question that plagued me was: *What the hell did I do to get here?* In this truly dark ballet of emotions, his punishment only increased my shame.

I think the only thing that got me to the other side was some of Herbie's spirit in me. His stories of hardship and suffering reminded me that life isn't fair, and you're going to be dealt some really hard blows. But so many of the wounds we nurse are self-inflicted, and the sooner we realize this, the better. Blaming others for our trials is a fool's errand. Taking responsibility, on the other hand, isn't just an errand: It is a completely new journey toward compassion, healing, and with any luck, wisdom.

The more time that separated me from my experience in The Ditch, the more my compassion for Sam grew. I remember thinking, *how shitty must his life have been, to take advantage of so many people.* Incidentally, I later learned that at the time Sam extorted me, his world was unraveling. By buttering up his lawyers, he found a viable, though fleeting, escape hatch from his complicated web of personal problems.

Translation: Sam was a Hot. Ass. Mess. And he was hurting. *A lot.*

But while I learned to have compassion for him, I also realized through therapy and self-reflection that it was not my job to take on Sam's burdens as my own. As a wise spiritual director once quipped, "not my monkey, not my circus." I had to make peace with the fact that Sam was facing *his* crucible, much as I faced mine. And while mine may have been punctuated by deep shame and self-loathing, his was an encounter with Justice.

A few months after I started The Bassett Firm, I met with the then-assistant General Counsel for the large national retailer I represented at my old firm. He was my contact, not my partner's, and so I felt confident asking him to send his work to The Bassett Firm. He was a taciturn man and I didn't expect him to show too much enthusiasm over my news of starting my own practice, but he did tell me that he'd heard about my fall from grace, the allegations others were lodging against me, and the unbecoming chatter in the industry. But he also said: "You know, Mike, people can make all the allegations they want. But until I see proof, I won't put any stock in them. So, you can have our work."

A similar incident unfolded that year, when I approached Todd Wright, a client I had represented for nearly twenty years. I told Todd that I was starting my own practice and I wanted to know if we could have his business. Apparently, my former law partner had visited him, even though he had never met this particular client or done any work for Todd. While I have no idea what was said during that meeting, I do know that Todd wasn't buying it. "That didn't sit well with me," he later told me.

I can't recall what else he said, but what I do know is that this interaction proved a resounding truth: *It's all about the relationship.* As my law partner and good friend Michael Noordsy is fond of saying: "You can't wait until the Friday before prom to ask a girl to go with you." My relationship with Todd was years in the making and ran so deep that even my flame-out did not deter him.

These inexplicable events rank right up there with the banker giving us a line of credit. Think of a major American corporation sticking by someone who had previously been under investigation by the FBI. It makes absolutely no sense. That is, unless you think about the role of Grace.

Grace, mercy, and loyalty.

After the meeting with Todd, I flew back to Dallas and opened File #162 for The Bassett Firm. On our nineteenth anniversary, February 4, 2021, we opened File #3,360.

I have no idea why, but that God seems to smile upon lawyers and fools.

Chapter 8:
The Halfway House: Halfway between the Crucible and Redemption

"Before the truth sets you free, it tends to make you miserable."

~ *Richard Rohr,* **Falling Upward:
A Spirituality for the Two Halves of Life**

I first set foot in the Halfway House on Monday, January 13, 2003, clad in a pair of black Levi 501s and a red, long-sleeved thermal shirt. It's funny how some of the most impactful moments in our lives–like the Judge's precise words to me at my federal sentencing hearing–elude us, but yet we remember minute details like what we wore. Add that to the growing list of Things I Will Never Understand.

The Halfway House was located in the small town of Wilmer-Hutchins, just a few miles from our home. And don't let the "house" moniker fool you: To quote the kids these days, the place was institutional *A.F.* It was set up much like a nursing home, with four "wings" and shared rooms. We ate lackluster, bulk-made meals together in a cafeteria-style hall and shared small cinder-block rooms and bare-bones bathrooms with as many as six other residents. If I wanted to talk to Liz or the boys, my only option was placing a collect call using the hall phone, often with a long line of impatient residents congregating behind me, awaiting their turns.

The 200-odd occupants of the House could be lumped into two main groups: individuals fresh out of federal prison (typically for non-violent drug-related crimes), and people like me, serving a mandatory sentence for some type of white-collar offense. I met a few interesting people, but I knew from the start that I wasn't there to make friends or find pen pals. This wasn't a chapter of my life I planned to revisit, so if I could help it, I kept my head down and my mouth shut.

But there are still days where I find myself regretting that choice, and I'd be lying if I said this didn't involve just a little ego and a lot of judgment. Having been fortunate enough to make it out of The Ditch, one of the curses I came to realize in time is how The Ditch isolates us from those who are right there alongside us at the bottom. I'm not sure if any of my housemates will ever read this book, much less remember me. But I can only hope they had someone to help them scale the steep banks of The Ditch like I did.

Most of the staff were decent humans, but there were a few, in particular, who seemed high on their situational power. One short guy with a Napoleon Complex seemed determined to put me down at every turn. Somehow he found out I was a lawyer and he took delight in pointing this out whenever he could. Like when he was searching me for contraband (which he did frequently, and to no avail).

It was in this context that I was thankful for my ability to become a social chameleon. Not standing out. Not drawing attention to myself. And in a sad way, the trauma of my childhood actually paid off. I knew how to at least attempt to make everyone like me, even in the face of powerlessness. So, I found myself biting my lip often and channeling respect for, if not the position, the person behind it. It was humbling, but I was determined to do all I could to get through those ninety days. And at times, that meant laying down my pride, even to the point of smiling in the face of a dude who delighted in making me suffer.

Daily life at the House was routine and depressing as hell. My goal from the moment I set foot inside was to spend as little time there as possible, so I rose at 5:30 a.m. daily and hit the road for work by 6:00, often working until well past 6:00 p.m., or at least as long as I could push it without attracting unwanted attention from the House staff. It was truly therapeutic to step away from that place and into a routine that felt so healing in its normalcy. Outside the walls of the Halfway House, people were suing each other, lawyers were negotiating, parties were showing up to court, and judges were issuing rulings. It all felt so refreshing, expected, and predictable in a way it never had before.

Sadly, though, even the respite I found in my work was laced with bureaucratic barbs, constant reminders that I had screwed up. I wasn't free to come and go as I pleased, so I had to call the House staff as soon as I arrived at the office. I had to call if I left for any reason, even to grab a bite to eat or head to court, and I had to let them know when I was leaving for the day. If I stayed too late, I drew suspicion. If I went anywhere without notifying them, I faced serious disciplinary action. And then there was the most painful (and most obvious) punishment: I could not, under *any* circumstances, go home to Liz and the boys for *any* reason–a fact made especially excruciating by the reality that home was just twelve miles away.

The invasion on my personal privacy didn't stop there. Because so many of my fellow residents were recovering drug addicts, the staff would issue random drug tests and body searches. Occasionally, before heading to work, a staff member would stop me, order me to turn out my pockets, and search me. (And this was no TSA pat-down, either.) Another time, someone in our wing had broken protocol. I can't remember how. But what I *do* remember is being marched into the parking lot at 2:00 a.m., being chided as a group, and then being forced to clean the restrooms as the sun slowly rose. Apart from my initial fall from grace, I can think of few events in my life more humiliating than this.

There weren't many bright spots in my weeks, but Liz and the boys were permitted to visit a few times. These visits were marked by a lot of complicated emotions. It was good to see them, but my shame often threw a pall over our time together. After all, having your family see you in a federal prison halfway house isn't exactly the stuff of Hallmark movies. The strain on Liz and the boys was palpable. Liz was forced to shoulder the burden of raising two adolescent boys on her own, and my shame was an albatross for C.J. and Kyle. High school social circles aren't exactly inclusive and forgiving, so my flame-out was doing nothing to make them feel integrated into the social scene at their schools.

But, God love them, they kept showing up. I think that's what we are supposed to do. To keep showing up for our people, our tribe, even when they embarrass us, let us down, or make our lives harder than they really need to be.

On Sundays, I was allowed to leave the House for a few hours. Liz and the boys would pick me up for Mass and breakfast at Whataburger: two forms of religion in one day. I couldn't deny the sheer joy of escaping the House each Sunday morning, but the staff's rules didn't bend for religion: I had to bring back a copy of the church bulletin, which always struck me as odd. Who knows. Maybe they were really interested in the parish's weekly pancake dinners.

Our family outings were certainly a breath of fresh air. I'd never before appreciated the simple joy of a well-flavored, non-institutional meal. But I'd be lying if I said our reunions weren't initially a touch awkward. Navigating the conversation was like toeing a field of landmines. Conjuring small talk wasn't the easiest when I'd spent my past seven days among recovering convicts, and the last thing I wanted to do was cause static for Liz. Not to mention, by that point, I felt like I'd abdicated my ability to give anyone advice, so I decided not to interrogate the boys about their performance at school. We kept the topics lighthearted and I tried as hard as I could to ignore what I was convinced were accusatory stares from other diners. At both Mass and the restaurant, my time with my family was marred by the constant fear that *they all knew...they just knew.*

I told no one about my stay at the House except my in-laws and my team at The Bassett Firm, but just like our Sunday outings or my sons' social lives, I knew that everyone *knew.* I knew from the number of unreturned phone calls, by the accusatory stares of strangers on my rare trips to a restaurant or store, and by the lawyers who pretended they didn't know me. I also knew our neighbors must've been curious when my truck wasn't parked outside our home for ninety days. In a small town, people figure things out, and I quickly became aware that my sentence was my public penance, my no-longer-secret shame, a giant, scarlet A on my chest...only mine was a scarlet D.A.: *Dumb Ass*.

When Liz and the boys dropped me off at the House after breakfast on Sundays, my heart would sink to the pit of my stomach. The stilted conversation may have been tough, but the excruciatingly long afternoons at that damn Halfway House were far worse. (You see, I could leave the Halfway House on Saturdays to go to the office and work. But not on Sundays.)

We weren't permitted outside (not that the parking lot was very enticing, anyway), so to pass the time, I read, slept, and worked in the kitchen. The best I could do was stay occupied until I could leave for work again at 6:00 the next morning, so I threw myself into any task I could find and willed the time to pass. And, as time seems to do when we constantly watch it, it moved at a glacial pace.

I missed Liz and the boys terribly, but I was also struck by the almost equal yearning for simple freedoms I'd taken for granted for more than three decades.

Traveling to a deposition.

Getting on a plane.

Going out to dinner.

Grabbing a mid-day coffee or sandwich.

Driving the scenic route just *because*.

Taking my own prescription medications instead of standing before some prison staff member who counted the pills and eyed me as though I was surely up to no good.

I think so many of us felt a similar yearning during the initial months of the COVID-19 pandemic: aching to just step outside without fear. And in another sadly helpful way, my time at the Halfway House primed me to never, ever take basic individual freedoms for granted.

My departure day was Friday, April 11, 2003: ninety days after I'd first set foot inside. Easter was just a week later, which meant I'd spent the entirety of Lent–a penitential, spiritually intense season for Christians–at the Halfway House, and my release coincided with the most significant event in the Church calendar. At the time, this was lost on me. I was too focused on just getting out. But in retrospect, I realize that there is no way that could've been an accident.

My bags were packed the night before and I planted myself in the lobby at 5:30 a.m. By 6:02, I steered my truck out of that parking lot for the very last time. As I turned onto the main road, I thought of a neuropsychologist friend's fascination with "closing pathways," that is, completing an act that feels unresolved. In my case, I knew that I needed to close my own pathway by taking the very same route home that I'd taken to get there ninety days prior. I knew that if I didn't close that loop, it would remain an open wound that would never truly heal.

But more importantly, there was something ceremonial and almost defiant about it, like a metaphorical middle-finger to those who thought I couldn't make it. So as I pulled out of the lot, I rolled down my window and jubilantly extended my *literal* middle finger, my triumphant gesture of defiance and celebration.

I was no longer the Man in The Ditch. He had been broken down. He had been transformed. He had been redeemed. Mike Bassett 3.0 had arrived, and he was ready to fight to the death for all that was good, true, beautiful, and meaningful. Scarred? Yes. Deterred? Not even.

And so close the loop I did–by rolling through every stoplight in that sleepy town, music blasting from my truck's stereo. I still remember the song. It was "Times Like These" by the Foo Fighters. And I still can remember singing at the top of my lungs with tears running down my cheeks:

> *It's times like these you learn to live again*
> *It's times like these you give and give again*
> *It's times like these you learn to love again*
> *It's times like these time and time again*

Have you ever felt that a song was written just for you? That it captured *exactly* what you were going through? Well, that's what this song meant to me that early Spring morning with the wind whipping my face and a new hope taking root in my heart. My life would never, ever be the same again.

And at the thought, I broke into what seemed like the first real smile in two years. And I couldn't stop.

Chapter 9:
An Ode to the Norman
Rockwell Life

The greatest glory in living lies not in never falling, but in rising every time we fall.

~ Nelson Mandela

There's nothing like a homecoming from a federal prison halfway house to make a workaholic grind to a screeching halt. Work could wait. So instead of steering my truck toward Dallas, I spent the entire day on Friday at home, as the kids say, *just chilling*.

You never really understand the rich luxury of simple joys–like a clean bathroom, a comfortable bed, and decent food–until you've been deprived of them, so I spent most of my time relishing the simple pleasure of being home. *My home.* In private, with the three people I loved the most in the world, with a decent meal and nary a skulking Halfway House employee in sight.

But while Friday was a day of true rest, Saturday was for celebration. Liz threw a homecoming party in our backyard with an intimate group of friends and family. The entire team from The Bassett Firm was there, along with Jim Stanton and our parish priest. We'd hosted a lot of parties at our home, but this one was different. The grass seemed greener, the flavors more vibrant, the beer colder, the laughter sweeter. It was as though everything around me simply burst with color and life. It was like a small-town-Texas rendering of a Norman Rockwell painting, one you'd see and say, "I want to be there. I want to *be them*." And for the first time in a long time, I didn't want to be anywhere else– or *be* anyone else.

The party symbolized the completion of this penitential chapter of my life: I'd done everything I *had* to do. I'd cleared the last hurdle, checked off the last item on the *I effed up* list. Now, I knew I faced a long, uphill battle to out-hustle other lawyers and build my reputation back piece by piece. So, I continued to lean on my faith for strength and guidance. I soaked in all I could from the Jesuits and attended Mass every Sunday, which seemed much richer now, with its centuries-old liturgy, predictable cadence, and the overwhelming knowledge that the celebration was the same everywhere, in every language, at every point in history. The Church was a stanchion of faith, security, and peace, and I didn't stray far from it.

When I say I'd become Mike 3.0, I mean this in the most radical way. Because not only had I become a different person: I became a different *lawyer*. It wasn't that I didn't tolerate bullies or suffer fools. I suddenly understood them. How much they must have been hurting. And the fear I once felt when trying cases was gone. Instead of feeling aflutter with nerves, I stepped into courtrooms with a new, steadfast confidence. After all, what was a jury going to do to *me* that I hadn't already done to myself?

This new worldview was liberating.

My time in The Ditch was like a refiner's fire that melted away my hard edges. Though I'd softened in many ways, my foundation was stronger. Humility became a new set of clothes I learned to wear more often, and the judgment seat I'd previously occupied was relegated to a corner of the garage. I worked hard to reclaim my reputation as a solid person and a stellar attorney. I took any and all speaking engagements I could find, and while I knew I had ground to make up, I also knew from my days in the law school library that I could out-work just about every other lawyer. So I did. And now when I look out my office window at the Dallas skyline, I realize that this nose-to-the-grindstone approach (Herbie and Sterling Bassett style) bore fruit.

At the same time, there was still much healing that needed to happen. I knew I couldn't control what people thought of me, but the unreturned calls and turned backs still stung. Even today, I feel flashes of insecurity, as I know there are some in the industry who remember my downfall and haven't quite recovered their confidence in me. But as Herbie used to say, "ninety-five percent of people don't give a shit about you, Michael. They've got their own stuff to deal with."

And he was right.

In my own mind, my downfall is the most deplorable thing anyone could have done. But I've learned that others–especially those who themselves have spent time in The Ditch–don't care nearly as much as I imagined they would. And though there are still plenty of lawyers who turned their backs on me and never re-entered my life, I've channeled the Ignatian wisdom of "benign indifference:" I simply won't waste my mental energy worrying about the state of someone else's heart.

There is so much I want to do. So much I feel *called* to do. So why spend time trifling over what I simply *can't* control when what I *can* control could make the world a better place?

Chapter 10:
Plugging into the Power Source

Make me a channel of your peace
Where there is hatred, let me bring love
Where there is injury, Your pardon Lord
And where there's doubt, true faith in You

~ Prayer of St. Francis

My release from the Halfway House was a watershed. At this point, I knew the debt I had to pay was done, satisfied, cleared. But my future remained uncertain at best, and I knew I had lots of work, growth, and healing yet to do.

Knowing I had my work cut out for me, one of my first acts as Mike 3.0 was to embark on a three-day silent retreat at the Montserrat Jesuit Retreat House just North of Dallas on Lake Lewisville. To say this retreat was life changing would be the understatement of the century.

Father Joe Tetlow was the Director of that Retreat House when I attended for the first time and we have remained close friends ever since. He is a rock star in the Jesuit community and has been my unofficial spiritual director for nearly two decades. Even now, well into his nineties, he still has time to share a meal or visit with me, either over the phone or in person. My introduction to Father Joe led me to fall in love with Jesuit spirituality, and during that time I came to learn that the Jesuits are all about action: how to take Christian morality into the marketplace. I rely on their wisdom and practices day-to-day in running my Firm, and their tools have proven just as useful as my legal training.

That weekend of my first retreat was unlike anything I'd ever experienced. There was a routine to it, but unlike the institutional grind of the Halfway House, it was a healing, comforting, soul-nourishing routine. From my arrival on Thursday night until my departure at noon on Sunday, we remained in absolute silence. We rose at dawn for morning prayer, ate breakfast in silence, sat through two spiritual formation talks in the morning, broke for a silent lunch, then enjoyed two more talks and evening Mass. It was a privilege that has only become more glaringly obvious with time.

During our daily downtime, the retreat leaders gave us activities to complete. One that I remember distinctly was a version of *Lectio Divina*, a Catholic spiritual practice that involves intense and focused reflection on a short passage from Scripture. The task is to tie a scriptural story to an experience in your own life where you encountered God.

The story that we were given was from the Gospel According to Matthew, Chapter Eight. Jesus was traveling with his disciples by boat and decided to lie down and rest when suddenly, a massive storm ravaged the boat. The disciples were terrified and begged Jesus to save them. He admonished them for their lack of faith before calming the raging seas. The passage struck me so intensely because I felt like I was in the boat. And yet unlike the disciples, I knew I was facing waves of my own making. Reading the passage, I felt every bit of their fear, but with the added shame of knowing that *I'd* created this storm. And when it came to calming the seas, I wasn't running to the resting figure of Jesus to ask for help: I was relying on my own brute force, my own foolishly perceived ability to silence the storms and right my boat.

But I also knew, in that moment, that this story was foundational to my faith for a reason. This reality had to be true: God *would* calm the seas, no matter what (or who) had incited the waves. He *would* steady my boat. And even if the waves were of my own making, the same God that calmed the angry seas would quell the storms in my life. I've since clung to this touchstone, through every hurdle and challenge. And I clung to it yet again when a global pandemic shook so many of us to our very foundations.

The silence and stillness of those three days changed me to my core. I entered the retreat center on that Thursday evening a far more judgmental, jealous person–transactional, cold, brusque. But when I left, I felt two or three zip codes' distance from the person I was. Of course, growing in virtue is a lifelong feat and one weekend cannot permanently reshape a heart that is forty-two years in the making–but I really believe that this retreat catalyzed a change that would make my old self virtually unrecognizable.

The only reason this worked, though, was because I had been broken. This intense immersion into the classroom of silence, into one-on-one encounter with the living God I believed in and trusted, into an environment reverberating with the energy and influence of the Jesuits and their way of life, would not have had the same impact on Mike

1.0. To truly open ourselves to radical transformation, I think we first need to be stripped to the studs, exposing the stuff we're really made of, the raw material with which God is working. And having just emerged from the Halfway House, I was as raw as they come, humbled and laid bare to the point that I was ready, willing, and able to be radically reshaped.

Spending three days in absolute silence, focused only on healing and reflecting on Truth, so drastically changed me that I've made these silent retreats an annual event: only now, I attend eight- or ten-day retreats instead of the immersive long weekend experience that was my gateway into Jesuit spirituality. These retreats are open to everyone, certainly not just practicing Catholics, and in my time there I have connected with people of all faiths: Muslim, Jewish, Buddhist, and Evangelicals. I truly believe that the experience of a silent retreat can tremendously benefit every living, breathing person. After all, imagine taking a few days each year to plug into a massive power source. Each time I do it, it sets into motion a series of seismic shifts in my life. And just when I think I've learned all I need to know about humanity, life, God, sin, virtue, and growth, I'm stripped bare once again.

It's painful. But it is fantastic.

Chapter 11:
The World Outside The Ditch

"Our Limitation is God's opportunity. When you get all the way to the end of your rope and there ain't nothin you can do, that's when God takes over."

~ *Denver Moore,* **Same Kind of Different As Me**

My time at the Montserrat Retreat Center, and in fact, all of the retreats I attended in those early years after my flame-out, provided emotional and spiritual sustenance. The wisdom shared by Father Joe and the other Jesuits, along with the various priests at our parish, Holy Trinity Catholic Church, continued to shape and mold me, shifting the paradigms by which I ordered my decisions, values, and behavior. Less judgment. More compassion. More silence. More service. Less arrogance. A posture of accepting my own limits and realizing that it was *through*, not in spite of, my brokenness that I was going to make an impact through the way I lived my life.

To this day, the lessons I have learned in my nearly twenty-year journey with the Jesuits continue to shape my life. Recently, I was looking back at notes I made on a return flight from Rome to Dallas in October of 2015. Liz and I were returning from our first pilgrimage with Father Joe, where we followed the footsteps of St. Ignatius from his birth place in Loyola, Spain, to where he died in Rome. Here were some of my thoughts that Tuesday afternoon:

- *It is because of–and through–my brokenness that God has called me to do my life's work.*

- *Always assign the most generous of intentions to others' actions.*

- *Communication–grounded in true humility–can soften the hardest heart.*

- *Life's road is strewn with many rocks and most of them are not mine. Leave them where they lie.*

- *Life is a pilgrimage and there are going to be detours and setbacks along the way.*

- *Give God a reason to forgive those who hurt you or are your enemies.*

My job is to love all of the people God puts in my life.

To me, spending time in silence with God is like plugging into the world's most powerful supercomputer. Every time I attend a retreat (whether it's for three days or ten), it reorients my life in a new direction. In a better direction. And hopefully, it makes me a better version of myself each time.

And let me be crystal clear. The thoughts you just read following my October 2015 pilgrimage? I drop the ball on all of those. Daily, in fact. I often assume the worst in people. Sometimes my words are not cloaked in humility, but are sharpened by anger. There are times I lose my cool when things don't go just as I planned. I have held grudges and I am not proud of it. And Lord knows that I often don't love everyone He puts in my path.

But here's the deal: It's not about doing it perfectly and never failing. It's about striving, daily, to be a better version of myself than I was yesterday. Perfection ain't the goal.

And what's more, I would be lying through my damn teeth if I told you life was all rainbows and sunshine as soon as I emerged from The Ditch. Some days, I felt the intoxicating thrill of traction, of forward progress. Others, I felt I was moving backwards at light speed. The specter of being "found out" still sat heavily on my conscience, and unfortunately for me, it didn't take much sleuthing for the big players in my industry to "find out."

At that time, one of our clients was a large corporation I had represented since 2002. Our point of contact was a man (let's call him Don) who was essentially the "Sam" of their company. In a way that was eerily similar to Sam, Don was a renaissance man, a brilliant but quirky and utterly magnetic individual. The first time we met, Don was impressed by the impactful brevity of my proposed opening statement for a particularly high-stakes trial, and thus began a long, mutually-beneficial relationship.

Shortly after I left the Halfway House, I was sitting in a deposition when my Blackberry vibrated in my pocket. It was an email from an insurance adjuster I had known for years. He just so happened to handle the claims for this large corporation, and he had forwarded me a message one of his fellow claims adjusters received from a Dallas lawyer. The lawyer's name was mercifully redacted, so to this day, I have no idea who sent it. But essentially, the email clearly showed that this lawyer had dug up some dirt and "outed" me not only to this insurance professional but also to Don. I had to take a break from the deposition as I found myself in a full-blown panic attack.

After I got myself somewhat back together, I returned to the deposition and tried to focus on the job at hand. It was only after the deposition was over, some five hours later, that I called Don's assistant. I had come to know her well and, interestingly enough, she would eventually end up taking Don's job.

With a dry mouth and my heart pounding in my chest, I told her the whole. Damn. Story. *All over again.* This was the first time I'd ever spoken of my flame-out to Don's assistant who, as far as I was aware, knew nothing about it. She listened and didn't interrupt. She thanked me for giving her the heads up. She said she'd visit with Don and "see what he wants to do."

When I hung up the phone, I felt like I had jumped out of a plane only to wonder whether I'd remembered my parachute: I was in free-fall until I finally heard back from Don's assistant, who relayed the glorious message that Don was entirely unperturbed by my explanation.

In fact, it seemed he all but totally dismissed the issue. Like Todd Wright and my faithful TBF staff, Don simply didn't care. He knew my character. He knew my work ethic. And with a multi-year relationship undergirding our work together, he needed more than my past acts of jackassery to disrupt what we had going for us. To this day, I still handle that corporation's business and neither that email nor my idiocy have been discussed again.

Another free-fall episode unfolded in 2003, when our Firm started representing a large poultry manufacturer. This client was a defense lawyer's dream. The client's "Sam" was a guy we'll call Tom. He was a demanding connoisseur of legal services, but once you earned his trust, he was loyal–and he showed his loyalty by sending us heaps of work. Once, an injured worker sued this client for head injuries he allegedly suffered when he fell off a ladder on a job site. We defended the client against the claim which, on its face, had little merit.

As it turns out, this Plaintiff had quite the rap sheet, with a propensity for committing serious felonies. His attorney designated an economist who attempted to make the case that the effects of the Plaintiff's head injury were torching his future job prospects. Notably absent from his report was any connection between a felonious history and the challenges the Plaintiff would face in securing employment. When I deposed the economist, I reviewed his model and assumptions in tandem with the Plaintiff's criminal history. I asked him if he was aware of the Plaintiff's criminal record, whether he'd considered the connection between a long rap sheet and difficulty finding a job. Surprise, surprise: He hadn't.

But before arbitration, the Plaintiff's attorney struck back. He filed a response pointing out that I, the defense attorney, *also* had a federal criminal record and as such, had no place castigating the Plaintiff for his. And so, there it was. My flame-out, forever memorialized in the annals of Texas personal injury filings.

Seeing my fall from grace referenced in an official legal document is definitely up there with the more shameful moments of my life, and as luck would have it, this also meant I had an obligation to explain my situation to Tom. Once again, though, the person whose opinion I so greatly feared was unperturbed at worst, utterly dismissive at best. Tom waved off my unbecoming past like it was a pesky mosquito at a barbeque. In fact, he later confided that he thought the attorney's filing revealed an utter lack of professionalism and an unprecedented level of assholery.

For the record, the Plaintiff was awarded zero dollars at arbitration. And I would be lying if I told you that I didn't grin from ear to ear when I read the arbitrator's ruling.

As you would expect, though, things didn't always work out so serendipitously. Five years after I emerged from The Ditch, we lost a large transportation client when opposing counsel engaged in a nasty little mud-slinging game. When I tried to point out the incongruity of the Plaintiff's story with her social media presence (one that showed that she was not, in fact, as gravely injured as her filings would indicate), her counsel fired back by calling the Risk Manager of the trucking company directly, telling him of my self-inflicted fall from grace, and how I was hypocritical for accusing his client of not being forthcoming.

This Risk Manager was not like Don or Tom. He dropped me–and fired our Firm–like a bad habit. This wasn't a big client, but it *was* steady, consistent work. And it was in the trucking world, which is a small one where news travels fast. In my mind, I could not help but feel like this fallout affected my other business. But there was no way to know for sure.

All this is to say, there were ups and downs, peaks and valleys. I felt alternately validated, then torn down, then uplifted again. The dips and peaks showed up in our Firm, too. At one point, in 2003, we had just enough funds, including receivables, to keep the Firm afloat for less than sixty days. This is a terrifying reality for a law firm. And of all the people who have shuffled in and out of our doors, it was having to cut loose a stellar paralegal named Mark Young that still puts a bad taste in my mouth. When we had to let him go, I felt as though I'd ruined his life and disrupted his promising career. But thanks to another set of small miracles, we were able to hire him back two years later, and to this day he is the most senior member of the Firm aside from me and Liz. Plus, he knows more than most lawyers about how to defend big, bad cases.

If 2003 was a year of grinding, 2004 made the 2003 team look like a bunch of slackers. We worked so hard that at times, I felt like I was pushing a boulder up the Sisyphean hill. But this hustle and grind never stopped. After all, you can liken running a business to dating. It's easy to get a girl to go to coffee with you. But staying married to her for thirty-eight years? Now that is a whole different level of commitment. You have to be intentional about your relationships in order to keep them, or else you open the door for other people to swoop in and claim them. And that's how we ran our Firm: constantly working as hard as we could to not only provide exceptional legal work, but also, to let our clients know they could trust us.

In fact, to this day, I attribute our survival (and, dare I say, success) to one thing: nurturing relationships. It's all about those day-to-day touches, those calls, cups of coffee, and dinners. To the trust that is built over time and through weathering challenges together. To showing up, again and again, to offer only your best, even when you don't feel like it, or want to hide, or your past embarrasses you.

That's why I've chosen to focus not on the lawyers who've slighted me or turned me down, the business I've lost or the people who've tried to take it, but rather, how I can right *my* relationships. And though "it" is still in the back of my mind, I've chosen to press forward.

Just a few months ago, I was rejected for membership to a national legal organization: a rejection that smelled suspiciously like someone had gone on a fishing expedition on my past mishaps. But the difference between what I now call Mike 4.0 and Mike 1.0 (or even 2.0 or 3.0) is that it took me exactly thirteen minutes to get over it. The temporariness of those thirteen minutes was the result of two decades of serious inner work: tearing-it-back-down-to-the studs kind of work. And while it was–and is–grueling work, it has made for a happier life and healthier inner world.

When I was at the Halfway House, I was assigned a cubby where the staff would keep my car keys every night. I was given a circular piece of brass about the size of a half dollar with the number 048 stamped on it: my cubby number. I kept the circular piece of brass on my keychain for years as a reminder. As a reminder of what happens when you're not true to yourself. As a reminder that all of our choices have consequences. As a reminder of a place I never wanted to return.

When C.J. went off to college at the University of Texas at Austin, he came back one summer with 048 tattooed on his right arm. I recently asked him why he did that, and I'll never forget what he said.

"Because it's a reminder to me, dude, of how hard you worked and how you persevered and that sometimes, life isn't fair. But you have to keep pushing forward."

He even told me that he got the tattoo at a point in his life when he'd traveled some rocky roads, like I had. Those three numbers were a constant reminder to him that life owes you nothing, that you need to do the hard work to overcome your challenges, and that you and only you control whether you become a victim.

Kyle opted for the slightly more extreme approach. During his third semester of college out in Lubbock, he came home with a very visible neck tattoo. By that I mean not even a turtleneck would have covered it. When Liz and I asked him why he'd done something so bold (to put it lightly) his response was, "I never want to be beholden to someone who is so quick to judge others that 'this' is what disqualifies me." And as if to double-down, he went on to get his Master's in Poetry.

After talking to C.J. and Kyle, I couldn't help but reflect on what Herbie and Jean would have thought of my flame-out. Given Herbie's hardscrabble upbringing, I think he would not have been scandalized by the stupid decision I made. In his life, he faced trials infinitely more difficult than I could even imagine. Had he been alive during my fall from grace, I think he would have had one of his signature clear-eyed conversations with me, and it would have started with something like this:

"Michael, that was a stupid damn thing to do. But there's no use in crying over spilled milk. My question is: What are you going to do to take care of Liz and those boys? What are you going to do to show them the man I know you are?"

My mom would have wanted to talk about everything that happened. *Ad nauseum.* She would have wanted to know what I was thinking and was feeling. What Liz had to say. What it was doing to the boys. But she would have very likely listened to all of this and then called me back a few days later to say: "Michael, my heart breaks for all of you. You can't undo what you did, but you can sure work hard to create a better future for your family. You can do anything you set your mind to, honey."

I think that my makeup is really a blend between the two of them: hard-nosed wisdom, and grace. Always, always grace.

My late brother, Sterling, actually knew the details of my time in The Ditch. Like I imagined Herbie would have reacted, Sterling wasn't judgmental at all. He was very matter of fact and practical and hit me with the fundamental questions: *What was going to happen? What did he need to do? When would we know more?* He wasn't one to collapse into a display of intense emotion. His world centered around the here and now, the facts on the ground.

Even once The Ditch was in the rearview, there were still so many symbolic steps I knew I needed to take. Heeding Jean's sage advice to focus on caring for my family, I took Liz to the Highlands in Monterrey, California, a place we vacationed once before my fall and that we both adored. At the bottom of The Ditch, I was hit with the terrifying reality that I may never be able to take her there again, so as soon as I was able, I knew it was necessary.

Sitting 500 feet above the Pacific Ocean, listening to the orchestra of waves and seals while we took in all the flavors and sounds and scents of the coast, I could hardly stand the gratitude I felt for her encouragement to walk through the flames, endure the pain of growth and refinement, and emerge a better man. A better version of myself, made new every single day.

Chapter 12:
Showing My Scars: Taking the Story on the Road

In a futile attempt to erase our past, we deprive the community of our healing gift. If we conceal our wounds out of fear and shame, our inner darkness can neither be illuminated nor become a light for others.

~ Brendan Manning, **Abba's Child**

Ever since our fateful Starbucks meeting back in 2001, Jim Stanton continued to be one of my main cheerleaders. He knew the unvarnished truth about my past and never once flinched, never pulled back the reins on his support for me. In fact, for more than a decade, he repeatedly harassed me to share my story publicly–a prospect that frankly made me feel vaguely sick.

"You need to write a book," he urged. "People need to hear your story."

And while I believed in his sincerity, I loathed the idea.

For years, sharing my story beyond the confines of the tightly-knit Dallas legal community was the *very* last thing I wanted to do. But as is often the case, God–and life–had very different plans.

In early 2019, a plaintiff's lawyer I knew by reputation invited me to speak at a seminar. It was an annual conference attended by nearly 200 Texas attorneys. This particular meeting was the thirteenth annual, and they were expecting record attendance. I knew this could mean only one thing: They were looking for more than just a lineup of generic, lackluster speeches. They wanted barn-burners. I felt serious pressure as soon as he asked.

Nonetheless, I hesitantly agreed, under the impression that I would be speaking during lunch. Lunch speeches tend to be slightly lower-pressure (most often, people are less engaged with the speaker than tracking the dessert platter's journey around the room). I was not given a topic, or any direction for that matter, but was told to simply hold the date. The colleague who invited me encouraged me to discuss how the law impacts people's lives. It sounded vague and squishy to me, maybe a bit Dr. Phil-ish, but he insisted he wanted me to transcend technical legal talk. So once again, I agreed.

As the event date approached, however, this particular lawyer called me again. "Change of plans," he said. "You're the keynote now." A bit more pressure, to say the least. And once again, he provided the most unhelpful guidance: "Talk about something you think the audience needs to hear." I promptly shoved the talk to the mental back burner and resolved to think about it again in a few months.

That June, I traveled to Cambridge, Massachusetts, to participate in Harvard's Advanced Mediation Training program. The program was held on Harvard's grounds and it was a one-mile walk from my hotel to campus. (In fact, I often wish that Jean was still alive so I could tell her I "went to Harvard.")

Each day, I took the same route to class, and I came to deeply value this rare solo time to think and reflect. This particular year, I thought about my talk while I walked. About what the committee wanted me to say. About what the audience "needed to hear." About what, exactly, I could possibly have to offer. Throughout the course of that week, my thoughts progressed something like this:

Monday: *I should talk about something that really puts a bee in my bonnet, like judgmental people. People need to hear about why judgmental people are the worst. I think that could fill an hour?*

Tuesday: *Maybe I should focus more on lessons I've learned in my career. That would seem more authentic, more personal. Maybe that's what they want?*

Wednesday: *Maybe I can distill that a bit more and talk about important life lessons I've learned? I'll keep thinking about that.*

Thursday: *Ok, so I think I can narrow it down to these key life lessons. That sounds good. But wait...Will it make any sense without some kind of context? I'll need to somehow explain why I think these lessons matter, right?*

Friday:

Son of a bitch.

I'm going to have to tell my story.

This realization hit me so hard that I stopped dead in my tracks, coffee in hand, surrounded by college students traipsing toward class. My knees felt weak, and all I could hear was Stanton's voice in my head: *"The world needs to hear your story."* I felt like a petulant toddler who refused to eat his vegetables, put his shoes on, or clean up his toys. All I could think was a defiant, "NO. I am NOT ready. I will NOT do that."

And yet, at the same time, it felt...right. It felt like I'd suddenly found the single missing piece to a 1,000-piece jigsaw puzzle and snapped it into place, completing the seriously overcomplicated scene that looked so easy on the box.

It felt right, because it *was* right. It was what I needed to do. It was the right thing *to* do. What I was *called* to do. If Stanton's encouragement was a seed, then the conference's invitation was a siren call. And I couldn't dodge that call any longer.

I wrote my entire speech while in isolation on a ten-day retreat with Father Joe. This was the first time I brought a computer with me on a retreat–typically, the presence of electronic devices is strictly prohibited–but Father Joe knew the significance of the step I was taking. In fact, we met daily to discuss my progress. He and I would have daily Mass, and in lieu of a scripted homily, he would connect the day's readings to my life and encourage me to take my story in one direction or another.

It seemed so strange and anachronistic, sitting at that retreat center with my laptop constantly under my arm, whipping it out to type one more thought, one more note, one more life lesson learned. But if I've absorbed anything valuable in my decades as a lawyer, it's that when work has to get done, it gets done anywhere and everywhere, whatever it takes.

And so a few months later, I was climbing onto a stage, my hands shaking uncontrollably as nearly 200 sets of eyes darted my direction. I saw dozens of colleagues in the audience: plaintiff lawyers with whom I'd had cases, judges before whom I'd argued, and of course, in the back, Liz and the boys.

I have stood before roughly 180 juries in my career and made countless arguments to judges, but I'd never been more terrified than I was at that very moment. The temptation to leave, to flee to safety, shred that speech into smithereens, and hole up at home was overwhelming. But after the initial thirty-second fight to stay rooted rather than turning on my heel and running out of there like a bat out of Hell, I took a deep breath and started to speak.

"On Monday, February 4, 2002, The Bassett Firm opened its doors," I said. "I finally had my own law firm. It should have been a day of celebration."

Almost 200 sets of eyes. All on me. What the *hell* was I doing? But I continued:

"Instead, it was a day when all I could think about was if I was going to federal prison."

From there, it was as though the fog of nearly two decades of fear, anxiety, and shame lifted. I told them the whole story. And let's be honest: I'm a Texan *and* a lawyer, so for me, telling stories is easy. It was the same thing I did when I stood in front of twelve of my fellow Texans, urging them there is another way to look at the same set of facts, a different way to think, see, and understand. But this time, I was telling *my* story. The story of events so traumatic that they radically and fundamentally changed who I am. And if my two decades of work was cleansing, sharing my story freely was like a baptism. You simply can't bear your soul to that many people and emerge unchanged.

When I finished the speech, people didn't applaud. There was a *standing ovation.* Close to 200 pairs of feet, hands, eyes (many of them wet), and the din of cheers and applause. Just when I thought I could sneak out the back of the room and fade into anonymity, lawyers flocked to the stage, thanking me, wiping tears, telling me they'd walked through something similar, or their child had, or colleague, or parent. They thanked me for my humility. They told me they felt less alone. Best of all, I shook hands with the guy who invited me in the first place, the one whose directionless pitch gave me such serious anxiety.

"That was even better than I thought it would be," he said, shaking his head.

I looked at him, aghast. "You knew?"

The truth is, he did know. The whole time. In fact, he invited me because he wanted me to tell *this* story to *this* audience. *That S.O.B.*

"I just thought this was a story that needed to be told," he said, grinning.

That, my friends, is the Operation of Grace.

Since February of 2002, The Bassett Firm has grown. Into The Ditch and beyond, my staff have remained loyal and redoubled their efforts to keep moving forward and growing. We now have a team of fifteen lawyers and we employ thirty-two people. I sit on the boards of several legal organizations and regularly speak at national trucking conferences. As of the date I am finishing this book, we've opened case number 3,520.

And while all of these things are nice, they are not what I celebrate most. Instead, what I am most thankful for is the journey and what it taught me.

I am most thankful for how that experience changed the way I practice law and the way I live my life. Recovering from my time in The Ditch required a tremendous amount of work. And to this day, it still does. As Liz and I told our RCIA students at our parish, growing as a person is not a matter of punching your ticket, boarding the train, and never looking back. It is a wholesale commitment to a daily practice of learning, questioning, humbling ourselves, and becoming students of our own lives.

We are constantly being made new. And to be a person of character and substance, not to mention, a mature disciple of Christ, you need to buckle up and get ready to get your hands dirty. Read, ponder, do the deep work, look for the log in your eye. This path is not for the lazy. It is for those who are just strong enough, just humble enough, maybe even just a bit reckless enough, to say: "I show up today fully open to what life will teach me, how it will shape me, and how suffering will fundamentally alter me."

Chapter 13:
The Big Nine: Wisdom (and Scars), Straight from The Ditch

Everyone has a history. What you do with it is up to you. Some repeat it. Some learn from it. The really special ones use it to help others.

~ J.M. Green

When we encounter traumatic events in our lives, it seems to me that we have two choices: Give up or get up. And if we choose to get up, and if we learn anything from our traumatic experiences, we emerge radically changed. That was certainly the situation for me, except what changed wasn't my circumstances or my luck, my inherent skills, gifts, or talents. I wasn't suddenly a handsomer, richer, more likeable, more prosperous, luckier man. On the outside, I was the same Mike. Rather, what changed was how I saw the world.

And that changed absolutely everything.

There is so much that my experience in The Ditch taught me, but if I had to distill this colossal learning curve down to its fundamentals, I would point out nine lessons that are now stamped on my heart and mind. And while these lessons certainly apply to lawyers and other client-facing professionals, the bigger picture is that all of them, ultimately, shoot directly to the hearts of *all* who are afflicted with the Human Condition.

Lesson One: Gratitude

In April of 2003, I found myself shopping at H-E-B, a local grocery chain in Waxahachie, Texas–as routine an act as you can imagine. And yet as I steered my cart through the aisles, I found myself absolutely flooded with gratitude. It wasn't that the experience itself was inspiring or I felt privileged to have the funds to feed my family (which, of course, is a blessing not to be discounted), but it was my taste of sheer, uninhibited freedom. I realized how thankful I was to be standing in that grocery store, because throughout my ninety-day stint at the Halfway House, this simple act was forbidden. I didn't have free reign to grab a drive-through coffee, let alone wander the aisles of H-E-B: I had to call and let them know my every move. Every time I left for lunch. And when I got back from lunch. Every time I went to a deposition. And when I got back to the office.

Because for ninety days, my every move was restricted and subject to being prohibited. Because for ninety days, *I couldn't even go grocery shopping*.

Everyone–and I mean *everyone* – has so much to be thankful for. And when we express or experience this gratitude, it infuses our lives with meaning. It changes our outlook from one of fear to one of joy. The grateful person is, in my experience, a better listener, a stronger friend, more deeply honest, more thoughtful of his or her colleagues, and more determined to do right. And as I wheeled my full cart out of H-E-B that day, I realized: *This is who I want to be.* The person for whom the simplest act inspires deep gratitude and joy. That was the life I wanted to live. That was the story I wanted to tell.

Lesson Two: Grace

Before my incredibly bad series of choices in 2001, I used to think that if you took care of your business and worked hard, you could inoculate yourself from life's punches to the face. When Mike 1.0 would read about someone's fall from grace (a DWI arrest, criminal problems, law license issues, getting sued), he would silently think: *Well, this person obviously didn't take care of his business. If he had, he wouldn't find himself in this situation.*

In other words, I divided people into two groups: those who always did the right thing and therefore never got burned, and those who were *less than*–who were "losers"–and whose lack of capacity to do the "right" thing landed them in The Ditch.

Well, having been in The Ditch myself, I now see this fallacy for what it is: an absolute, evil lie. All of us, regardless of who we are, how we were educated and raised, and how intelligent we think ourselves, are one left-turn from The Ditch. Each of us has the capacity to make really good life decisions. To be incredibly noble and kind and generous and loving. But each of us also has the capacity to make really stupid decisions. To be mean-spirited and selfish and hateful.

This boils down to two words: *free will*. It is a blessing and curse. The ability to make our own decisions can lead us into incredibly rich and meaningful experiences, but it can also be our downfall. It's who we are, and how each of us is wired. It's what makes us human.

Now that I accept these truths, I see the world through different eyes. When I read about the lawyer who's been sued or disbarred, my first thought isn't, *well he surely brought this upon himself*. My first thought now is: *I've been there. And that could easily be me again tomorrow.*

While I am still a work in progress and often find myself tempted back into judgment, I've learned instead to don the cloak of compassion more often. And let me tell you: It's a much happier way to live.

Lesson Three: Redemption

On September 14, 2019, during an ESPN broadcast, a college student named Carson King held up a sign requesting donations for a beer supply. As luck would have it, his sign resulted in him receiving more than one million dollars in donations. King donated *all* the money (minus the cost of one case of beer) to an Iowa children's hospital.

King gained public acclaim for his charitable act. But as an unfortunate result of his newfound notoriety, the *Des Moines Register* dug into his background and exhumed two racist tweets that King had posted eight years prior while he was sixteen. Aaron Calvin, the investigative reporter, was tasked with making the ancient news public. Before the castigatory article was published, King held a press conference to express deep remorse for his indiscretions. But that wasn't enough for Anheuser-Busch, who had collaborated with King for the charitable donations. After the press conference, the company severed ties with King.

King's treatment didn't sit well with his many newfound fans. The *Register* was flooded with angry comments for bringing King's racist tweets to life. And to prove that we are all indeed one left-turn from The Ditch, it was discovered that the reporter, Calvin, had himself posted bigoted tweets in the past. Once this came to light, the *Register* promptly fired him.

This type of scorched earth approach to judging human character has many names. Frequently, it's cited as "cancel culture," a phrase that has since been hijacked by political tribalists on both sides of the aisle. Semantics aside, the larger problem this trend signals is the disturbing comfort with which many of us happily condemn (or defend) the mistakes of others. For a brief moment, we all get to play Lady Justice–except no one is making us wear a blindfold. In a matter of hours or news-cycles, a person can go from unknown quantity, to beloved philanthropist, to a monument of his most abject failure.

The reality, though, is that few of us ever occupy one side of this spectrum permanently. As philosopher, theologian, and social critic Cornel West once said: "Justice is what Love looks like in Public." And I think, in the best circumstances, he's right.

So the question is, when the Sword of Justice is drawn on us, do we want it to have been sharpened by love? Or by vengeance? I suspect that many of you already know the answer.

This shoots straight to the heart of an incredibly impactful truth: that we are all, ultimately, redeemable. Good people do really stupid things. And good people often do evil things. But none of us, no matter how egregious our flaws, stand beyond the healing light of redemption.

Lesson Four: Compassion

A reprint of Rembrandt's painting *The Return of the Prodigal Son* hangs in my office. It depicts the moment when the revenant son returns home and rather than facing scorn for his long absence, is met with kind embraces from his father. I ordered the largest print I could to remind myself to be like the father who, to the great chagrin of the "good" son in the story, welcomed his wayward son with open arms in spite of their tortured history.

In our day-to-day lives, we will inevitably interact with people who have wounded us. And while I am not suggesting that we let people walk all over us, Jesus himself exhorts us to offer the other cheek to those who strike us, to give them our tunics when they ask for our cloaks, and to walk two miles with someone who forces you to walk one. Perhaps this scriptural call isn't an invitation into weakness but tremendous strength–the strength of a person who knows how to overlook past transgressions.

Nelson Mandela said famously that "resentment is like drinking poison and then hoping it will kill your enemies." It's true. Being resentful doesn't change or impact the person you resent, but will slowly poison your mind, heart, and soul.

So, the next time someone wounds, rejects, abandons, accuses, or upsets you, think of the Prodigal Son. What would have happened if his father cut him off from the family? What if this story did not exist as an encouragement to all of us to see not just the flaws of others, but to acknowledge them as infinitely pardonable in the Father's eyes? What if every time we made a misstep, someone sat on a judgment seat to condemn us? Would we ever recover from that?

Having myself gone from accusatory judge to hapless accused, I can tell you that I would not have survived but for the compassion and grace extended by others. And it pains me to the depths of my very soul to share that I know of others who've been in my position and lacked that embrace of compassion.

They took their own lives.

I knew them, and their faces haunt me. How different would their lives have turned out if someone, anyone, had extended their arms in a welcoming embrace, like the Prodigal Son's father?

Lesson Five: Loyalty

When The Bassett Firm officially opened its doors that Monday morning in February, I gifted all four employees a paperweight with the word "LOYALTY" stamped on it. I gave it to them because they had chosen loyalty over money, over job security, over the mob's call to cast me off like the greatest villain the Texas Bar had ever seen.

Fast forward to November of 2019.

I was in trial, serving as local counsel for an out-of-state plaintiff attorney who sued a corporation for the wrongful death of a family patriarch. Our clients were the patriarch's two adult daughters. As fate would have it, our Firm had previously done work for the insurance company that insured the corporation.

On the first day of the trial, I assumed at least one of the several folks behind defense counsel's table was an insurance company representative. Sure enough, one of them was the Claims Manager from the insurance company for whom we'd worked. (I'd never met this person in the flesh, so I couldn't identify him by sight.) During a break, I checked my phone to find a voicemail from an adjuster with that insurance company, calling to refer us a new case. A big case. I returned her call and told her we'd be happy to help after I'd cleared any conflicts.

After clearing conflicts, at 4:02 p.m., the adjuster sent an email officially hiring our Firm. But at 6:04 p.m., this same adjuster sent an email explaining that she had just received a message "from Management" that our Firm was *not* being assigned any new cases because I was "lead counsel in a case against one of their insureds."

My role in the case was minor. Nonetheless, I was flattered that they viewed me as being just as significant to the case as lead counsel. As you can imagine, for the rest of that night and early the next day, I was consumed with this issue. *Were we going to lose this insurance company as a source of business? What should I do? Should I confront the Claims Manager and ask him what we could do to make it right?*

As is often the case, my wife's observations and wisdom quelled my burgeoning dilemma. Her text message the following morning read: "You need to remember you are local counsel for the family you are helping right now. I think it's important that you keep your focus on them."

Of course.

It was so simple. It was about loyalty. My present loyalty was to two women who had lost their father. Once I realized this, all of my anxiety dissipated, and I couldn't believe I'd been torn up by an issue that hadn't even existed twenty-four hours prior.

Knowing where our loyalties lie will save us from decisions that can create gaping chasms: not only between us and our professional colleagues, but even more seriously, from our families, from our communities, the lifeblood that supports and sustains us. I was immensely grateful that my wife pushed me to stay loyal to two bereaved women, which was my job, my duty, my responsibility at that moment. Life and business are not a zero-sum game, and we will always come across new opportunities to profit. But our duty to serve the people sitting right in front of us at a specific moment in time? That's a once-in-a-lifetime call.

Lesson Six: Humility

When I was young, I was ten-feet tall and bulletproof. In fact, even well into my mid-thirties, before I stood in front of a federal judge awaiting a sentence, my colleagues likely would have used the words "supremely self-confident" or even "arrogant" to describe me. And they were spot-on.

As a young lawyer, I hid behind the cloak of arrogance to conceal my own shortcomings. I used to believe that I could never confess my dirty little secret that I might not know what I was doing from time to time. I could never admit to myself–much less others–that there were lawyers out there who were far better at the practice of law than I was. So instead of equivocating, I would act out in egregiously unjustified self confidence and assure my colleagues and clients that *Mike's GOT this*.

But the good thing about the purification process of The Ditch is that it made me realize how little I really know. It made me realize that there are, and always will be, *many* lawyers out there who are far more skilled than I am at their craft. It made me realize that I can't hang my hat on being "the best." That I don't have all the answers. And the immensely freeing revelation is that *I don't have to.*

On July 30, 2020, after five months of what I can only imagine were a lot of stressful days and sleepless nights, Dr. Anthony Fauci put himself on the line in a way that is foreign to most of us: He agreed to throw the first pitch of the Major League Baseball Season–something I'm almost certain they don't teach in medical school. At my age, I'd like to think I could have made the sixty-foot, six-inch pitch. But to have the guts to do it at Dr. Fauci's age, which, at that time, was pushing eighty? That's surely another story.

But for all the awkwardness, Dr. Fauci stepped up to the plate (literally and figuratively) and gave it his all. And when it went poorly, did he blame his assistant? Did he blame the weather? Did he suspect foul play?

Certainly not.

Speaking to ESPN in a subsequent interview, Dr. Fauci chalked it up to his own failure to assess the distance of the throw. But it was his closing line that I appreciate most: "It was my bad all the way," he told the interviewer.

Think about how much better off we would be if we, too, acknowledged that often, our failures are "our bad all the way." That there's more we don't know than what we do know. That sometimes we don't get the measurements right.

After six decades on this planet and nearly four in legal practice, I can tell you this: It's liberating to respond to questions or challenges by saying, "I have no idea. But I will find out," or, "I really screwed that up. What can I do to make it right?"

Humility grows only in the strong spirit, in the person who knows who he is. It is the ultimate sign of strength–*not* of weakness or failure.

Lesson Seven: Tenacity

When the bottom fell out of my career in 2002, I had a choice to make: Throw in the towel or get up and move forward. And let's been honest– had it been up to me, I would have likely thrown in the towel. However, as I've shared, it was my wife who said to me shortly after it all blew up, as clear-eyed as a person can be: "You were meant to be a lawyer. And that's what you're going to do."

From that point on, I never gave up.

But let me be very clear. It was not as if the road was smooth from that point forward. To the contrary, the struggle was just beginning and there were many times I wanted to throw up my hands and say, "to hell with this. I'm done." But I kept plugging away. I kept grinding. Day. By. Day.

The question is not whether you'll fall down or get knocked down. That's inevitable. Life is going to punch you squarely in the nose. The question is, how you will respond when it's your time to be bloodied-up a bit? Will you blame others? Point to your circumstances? Or will you face the pointy end of the spear with tenacity and say, *I can figure this out. I can grow. And I will get through this and emerge a stronger person?*

Lesson Eight: Perspective

In a whirlwind of events that began with me wearing a pink shirt on Valentine's Day and boarding a Southwest Airlines flight where Colleen Barrett was a passenger, I ended up having lunch with Herb Kelleher, his assistant, and Colleen at Bugatti's Restaurant in Dallas. Having always been a fan of Herb's, I was anxious to pick his brain and learn some of The Master's secrets. So I asked him, "Mr. Kelleher, what can I do to be a better lawyer and run a better law firm?"

Herb took a drag of his ever-present cigarette and a long pull on a drink that looked an awful lot like a Bloody Mary and asked: "Mike, do you know the question I ask every day when I come in the office?"

I had no idea.

He said, "I ask, 'how many take offs did we have yesterday?' And then I ask, 'how many landings did we have yesterday?' If the numbers match, it's going to be a great day."

Simply put, Herb Kelleher knew how to keep things in perspective.

I think we would all do well to follow suit. Not every loss, error, mistake, or mishap is cause to wring our hands and declare it's all over. Do your take-offs match your landings? If so, does it really matter if there was some turbulence in between? If you ran out of coke and peanuts? If someone complained about the cabin temperature?

Surely not. After years of public shame and three months in a federal prison halfway house, I've learned to not cry over spilled milk–or its equivalent in my life or my law practice. Learning to keep those minor mishaps in their place results in a life rich with gratitude, not to mention, laser-focused attention on what really, truly matters...which, when you think of it, isn't a whole hell of a lot. Family. Community. Connection. Faith. Grace. Gratitude. Health. Fulfillment.

Perspective. Let's never forget it.

Lesson Nine: Community

On the morning of my personal judgment day–my federal sentencing hearing–I had breakfast with Liz and Father (now Bishop) Mark Seitz, one of my greatest spiritual mentors. Bishop Seitz shared a story with me. It was about King Nebuchadnezzar, who set up a golden figure and ordered all of his officials to bow down and worship it, or else he would order them to be thrown into a fiery furnace. Three brothers who held high office flatly refused to worship the golden idol. Not only did the King order them to be cast into the flames, but he commanded that the heat be turned up about seven times. Once the brothers were tossed into the furnace, the King looked down to see not three, but four figures inside: the three brothers, and a fourth figure that resembled the Son of God.

Bishop Seitz ended the story by looking me dead in the eyes and saying: "Mike, no matter what happens today, no matter what fire you are thrown into, *you will not be alone.*"

We are never, ever alone.

I think that some of us may succumb to the mindset that it all rests on us. We have collectively bought into this sort of rugged individualism that our country romanticizes. But this is a very dangerous way to think. When we think we are alone and have no one to turn to, we are easily swayed into poor decisions. That is certainly what happened to me. I knew what Sam was asking me to do was wrong. But I felt as though I shouldn't have to ask for help. Or perhaps I felt that if I had gone to my law partners or my family they would have thought less of me.

Regardless, I isolated myself and withdrew until I was utterly alone–which is never a good place to be. After all, watch how a pack of hyenas will take down its prey. The very first thing they do is separate the victim from the herd.

Whether you know it or not, you are surrounded by people who care about you. People you can turn to when things get dicey. People who are there to support you. And if you have to ask yourself if what you're about to do is right or wrong, stop. Turn to someone you trust. Ask them. Connect to your community.

Communion is the Source and Summit of the Catholic Faith. And while it signifies something sustaining for us spiritually as Christians–the Body, Blood, Soul, and Divinity of Christ–it is also about, well, *exactly* what it signifies: communion. We also call it the Body of Christ. One body, one Church, in spite of divergent beliefs, cultures, and backgrounds–we are all one. And part of that oneness is that all of us have been in The Ditch at some point. And if we haven't, we certainly will be before too long.

After all, we were never promised ease. Never promised we would sail through life unscathed. But we *were* promised that no matter what we endure, we will never, ever be alone. It's been said again and again, in slightly different ways, by wise people throughout the ages, but it bears repeating: The only way out is through. And the only way through is together.

Epilogue

Suffering has been stronger than all other teaching, and has taught me to understand what your heart used to be. I have been bent and broken, but–I hope–into a better shape.

~ *Charles Dickens,* **Great Expectations**

When I'm traveling by plane, I always have to laugh when the flight attendants ask: "Do you have any baggage?"

Do I have any baggage? *Do I?*

Oh, HELL yes, I do. Better free up some space in that overhead storage compartment, folks, because it's going to take up some room.

Everyone, and I mean *everyone*, has baggage. Some loads are heavier than others, filled with more years (or decades) of mistakes, mishaps, suffering, and shame, but we all carry our baggage with us. That much is inevitable. The question is, what will you do with your load? Will you collapse under its weight? Or, will you choose to fill your bags with the emotional, spiritual, and relational sustenance you need to weather life's inevitable trials? Will you choose to occasionally let others carry your load for you when you need a reprieve? Will you take up the loads of others when they need support and companionship?

Because to be someone who is strong and humble enough to help others shoulder their loads even when they are bending under the weight of their own? That is a currency that never fails.

My friends, at some point on your journey through life, you will find yourself buried by your own baggage, stripped bare at the muddy, craggy bottom of The Ditch. Most people know what it's like to struggle through life's long valleys, but The Ditch is different. The Ditch will break you, but in that brokenness lies the potential for raw and radical transformation.

So the real question isn't *if*, but rather, *how*. How will you emerge from The Ditch? No one can make that choice for you, but I have an unshakeable belief that our biggest mistakes can be the first steps towards a life of impact. In my case, The Ditch broke me, but it broke me so that the Jesuits–and their timeless values of peace, detachment, selflessness, and community–could fill me. I was a broken vessel. My shards drew blood–both my own, and from those I loved. But what healed me was something I'd never experienced before, at least in its pure and unadulterated and, dare I say, *countercultural* form:

Joy.

Happiness is the zeitgeist of our modern age, but I don't focus so much on happiness these days. Happiness in the eyes of our culture feels like a passive state, an emotion, an experience that can evaporate just as quickly as the triggers that sparked it in the first place. Instead, I strive for joy. And to me, that means being content with what I have and with where I am, regardless of how that appears on the outside. It is not circumstantial, transient, emotions-based, but lasting. Transcendent. It is witnessing the good fortune of those you love most. It is hot cups of coffee paired with a patient, listening ear. It is the smile in Liz's eyes. It is watching my sons persevere, again and again, in fighting their demons. It is sitting in silence for eight days and encountering, yet again, the glorious truth that I am a sinner, mercifully forgiven. And ultimately, it is a *choice*: a choice to live in a certain state, a state in which we actively *choose* to see the good in every circumstance, even when the world tells us it's time to throw in the towel and wallow.

The thing about The Ditch is that it is so universal, but each individual's experience within it is intensely personal. I believe that we are called to share our personal experiences in The Ditch so we can help other people discover the transcendent power of joy–the inexplicable joy of submitting ourselves to the lifelong process of sanctification. And while we may not be able to stop others from ending up in The Ditch, when they emerge, we *can* help them navigate the journey of slowly shedding lingering vestiges of that heavy wool coat of shame–the one that the world will try, again and again, to foist upon us all.

In the end, I suppose this is a story of hope. A story for all of us.

My hope for you is *not* that you will never suffer. Unfortunately, I cannot guarantee that, so I refuse to placate you with false promises. Storms *will* come, and you *will* be battered and bruised. Instead, my hope for you is that when you find yourself in The Ditch, you will trust that your suffering is slowly but surely molding you into a better, stronger person. Like clay in a potter's hand, each bit of pressure, pain, and disfigurement will smooth and shape you into a new creation. And when you make it through, you will be changed. You will choose to seek joy over waiting passively for happiness to land on your shoulder. You will embrace hard seasons instead of asking for the chalice to pass you by. You will see someone else in The Ditch and instead of passing righteously by, you will roll up your sleeves and climb down, knowing that it could just as easily have been you. And you will understand, to the depths of your soul, that no one–not a single one of us, no matter how far we've fallen or how distorted we've become by our own suffering–is beyond the healing reach of the Operation of Grace.

Thank you for letting me share my story with you. Peace be with you.

~ The Man in The Ditch

I will be likened to the raindrop which washes away the mountain; the ant who devours a tiger; the star which brightens the earth...I will build my castle one brick at a time for I know that small attempts, repeated, will complete any undertaking. I will persist until I succeed.

~ Og Mandino

Acknowledgements

As with every other accomplishment in my life, this book would have never happened without the help and support of quite a few people. To name all of them would result in an Acknowledgment longer than the book. But here is my stumbling attempt to give credit where credit is due.

First, thank you to Alexandra Davis for agreeing to help me write this book. You learned my voice and it shows in this book. Thank you for your incredible writing skills and even more impressive organizational skills. But for you this book would still be floating around as an unfinished idea.

Next, a huge shout-out to Jim Stanton, who not only stood by me when most fled the scene, but who was one of my biggest cheerleaders. You will never know, Stanton, how your faith in me was the only thing that kept me going some days. If I can be half the friend to others that you were to me, I will have done well.

Staci Cassidy, you showed me what loyalty and grace and humor look like. I will never forget how you were there in the early and very dark days. And without you, *The Man in The Ditch* never would have become our Firm Mission Statement–and the genesis of this book.

Thanks to Todd Wright for being a true friend who took a chance on me when no one else would.

To my dear, dear friend Dick Fallon–I will never forget how you were always in my corner, even when others would have nothing to do with me. And the Las Vegas trips will forever bring a smile to my face.

Thanks also to Martin LeNoir and Jim Burnham for your outstanding counsel and representation. Without you two and your tireless work, I would not have been able to continue practicing law.

To Bishop Mark Seitz who stood by me–literally–when it was all on the line. Your deep faith and compassion for me and my family are the best homily you have ever given (not that you haven't given some really good ones).

To all the Jesuits who have shaped my worldview and, hopefully, made me a better version of myself: Father Joe Tetlow, Father Ron Boudreaux, Father Anthony Borrow, Father Stephen Pitts, and many, many others. You all inspire me to continue to do the next good thing.

To my sons, C.J. and Kyle. Your worldliness and complete belief in me are still hard to believe and accept. From the day I went into The Ditch until today, you both have shown me what it means to be not only a good friend, but also a solid man.

And lastly, to my beautiful bride, Liz. Your belief in me–and your trust in God–are humbling to say the least. You *never* doubted me. You *never* let me even think about throwing in the towel. You stood by me from day one. You are *still* my rock in the storm